ANGELIQUE C. HAMANE

SELF-REPRESENTED

A Step-by-Step Guide to Contesting a Trust or Will Without a Lawyer

CALIFORNIA EDITION

Volume I: Filing the Petition

PRO PER PROBATE PUBLISHINGS | www.properprobate.guide

To the Unrepresented and Unheard,

For those who have been hurt, used, or manipulated—and have finally said, "No more." For those forced to navigate a legal system they never asked to enter, with no resources, no guidance, and no choice but to fight. This is for you. May it give you the knowledge and confidence to stand your ground and demand justice.

Copyright © 2025 by Angelique C. Hamane

All rights reserved. No part of this publication may be reproduced, stored in a retrieval system, or transmitted in any form or by any means—electronic, mechanical, photocopying, recording, or otherwise—without the prior written permission of the author, except in the case of brief quotations used in reviews, academic works, or scholarly references.

This publication is provided for informational purposes only and does not constitute legal advice. Readers are encouraged to consult a qualified attorney regarding their specific legal situation.

Pro Per Probate™ is a trademark of Angelique C. Hamane.

ISBN (Print): 978-1-968669-00-3
ISBN (e-Book): 978-1-968669-01-0

First Edition
Printed in the United States of America

For permissions, inquiries, or further information, contact:
info@properprobate.guide, www.properprobate.guide

Published by Pro Per Probate Publishings

Disclaimer

This book is not a substitute for professional legal advice. I am not an attorney, and the information provided is based on my personal experience navigating the probate process in California, specifically within the Los Angeles Superior Court system. Probate laws and court procedures vary by state—and sometimes even by county—so it's essential to confirm the rules and requirements that apply in your jurisdiction.

While this guide offers general information and practical strategies, it should not be relied upon as legal advice. If you have questions about your specific situation or need help interpreting the law, I encourage you to consult a licensed attorney or contact your local court. For readers who qualify, I've included information about free or low-cost legal aid resources at www.properprobate.guide.

Using this book does not create an attorney-client relationship, and I assume no liability for actions taken based on the content herein. Representing yourself in court is complex and challenging; this guide is intended solely to support you in navigating that process to the best of your ability.

Table of Contents

Welcome	ix
Prologue: Background	xiii
Part I: Understanding Probate	xv
Chapter 1: Understanding Probate	1
Chapter 2: Steps Toward Trial: A Brief Roadmap	21
Part II: Before Filing a Petition	43
Chapter 3: Understanding Deadlines	45
Chapter 4: Who Has Standing?	57
Chapter 5: Do You Have a Strong Case?	67
Chapter 6: When You Might Be Doing This Alone	81
Part III: Filing a Petition	93
Chapter 7: Overview of the Filing Process	95
Chapter 8: Legal Content of the Petition	105
Chapter 9: Legal Grounds for Contesting a Trust or Will	133
Chapter 10: Procedural Requirements	163
Chapter 11: The Final Step: Filing Your Petition	211
Epilogue: What Happens After Filing a Petition	227
Acknowledgements	231
About the Author	233
Glossary of Terms	235
Legal Grounds and Related Codes	241

References 243

Case Law 245

List of Tables and Figures 247

Final Thoughts: Moving Forward with Confidence 251

Welcome

Welcome to *Self-Represented: A Step-by-Step Guide to Contesting a Trust or Will Without a Lawyer*.

If you're reading this, you're probably where I was a few years ago: angry, frustrated, and maybe feeling a little desperate. Maybe you've just learned that you've been unfairly cut out of an inheritance. Maybe someone close to you took advantage of a vulnerable family member, and now they're walking away with everything. And maybe, like me, you've realized that hiring a lawyer just isn't an option.

Let me tell you how I got here.

After my mother died in February of 2022, my siblings and I were still deep in grief when we received a Notification of Trust Administration. We'd been disinherited. One of my brothers was named as the sole beneficiary. We were shocked, furious, and determined not to let him get away with it. Hoping for some kind of path forward, we went to see a lawyer.

We were referred to two lawyers who specialized in litigation. They agreed to meet with us – telling us that they charge $350/hour. We created a Word document that summarized our claims and evidence, and spent an hour with the lawyer. We guessed our mother's estate was worth around $1.5 million, but without proof, it was just a rough estimate. After meeting with lawyers, they decided not to take our case. They explained that pursuing the case would cost so much in legal fees and court expenses that, by the end, it might not be worth it.

By the time we got the bill—$3,555 for that initial meeting—we were stunned. It was clear we couldn't afford to hire an attorney. Trapped between not qualifying for free legal aid and not being able to afford professional help, we felt defeated and abandoned, trapped in a system where justice seemed reserved for those who had money.

But here's the thing: for us, this fight wasn't really about the money. It was about *principle*.

This was the second time we'd been burned by the same brother. Years earlier, he had convinced our father to sign over a four-unit property to him. He "bought" it for $150,000—a fraction of its value by taking over the $104,000 mortgage, borrowed against the property to pay the difference, and then eventually sold it for $1.9 million. None of us challenged him then. We stayed quiet, tried to keep the peace, let him walk away with that fortune. He counted on us to stay silent again.

This time, we couldn't let him get away with it. We didn't have the money to hire a lawyer, but we knew we had to do *something*.

That's when we decided to do it ourselves.

This book is the resource I wish I'd had back then. It's not here to make promises or replace real legal counsel, but it *is* here to give you the basics you'll need to navigate probate court without a lawyer. I won't sugarcoat it—self-representation is hard.

Probate law is full of technicalities and traps. But if you're determined to stand up for what's right, and hiring an attorney just isn't an option, this guide will give you a place to start.

One thing to keep in mind: This guide is based on my experience in California probate court, specifically Los Angeles Superior Court. Each state—and sometimes each county—has its own set of probate rules and procedures, so if you're reading this from another location, be sure to check your local court rules. Many probate processes are similar, so this book can still help you understand the basics and show you what to expect but always confirm the specific rules for your jurisdiction.

If you do qualify for legal aid, I encourage you to explore that option first—there are resources available for those who meet the criteria, and I've included some information in my website at www.properprobate.guide to help you find support. But if you find yourself in that same middle ground we did, caught between high costs and limited options, this book is here for you.

Let's get to work.

Prologue: Background

I come from a large family—I have seven siblings, one of whom is deceased. When my mother passed away, we were still processing the loss when we received a notice that we'd all been disinherited. All of us, except for one brother, had been completely cut out of her estate.

My brother's manipulation of our mother's finances and decisions began years before she ever signed the trust. In 2013, he convinced her to sell her home under the pretense that he would take care of her, but shortly after, he began isolating her from the rest of the family and took control of her finances. At the time of that sale, and without notifying any of us, he disposed of family heirlooms—including a baby grand piano—along with memorabilia like yearbooks, childhood photographs, and valuable jewelry. Then, nearly two years later, in 2015, just one month after she was diagnosed with end-stage renal disease (ESRD), he persuaded her to execute a living trust. That same month, he moved her into a senior living facility.

According to the trust's Schedule A, she intended to place all her assets into the trust, including her home, savings, investments, and other items. However, after her passing, we discovered that the trust was nearly empty. While we still lack a complete financial accounting, we believe he systematically used her assets for his own benefit, including commingling finances and using her money to purchase his home, cars, and business equipment in her name.

Faced with these revelations, we felt we had no choice but to fight back.

We believed our brother had exercised undue influence over our mother, and that she lacked the capacity to understand the full consequences of the decisions he pushed her to make. Our petition argued not only lack of capacity and undue influence but also financial and elder abuse, as we believed he had manipulated her assets and isolated her from the rest of the family.

With no money for a lawyer and no one else willing to take on our case, we made the decision to represent ourselves. This guide is the result of that journey—a resource I wish I'd had when I was trying to navigate probate court on my own.

PART I

Understanding Probate

Before filing any paperwork, it's important to understand how probate litigation works. This section provides an overview of probate, key players involved, and how contested cases move through the court system. Knowing what to expect will help you navigate the legal process with confidence.

CHAPTER 1

Understanding Probate

Introduction

When a loved one passes away, their **estate**, which includes all their property, assets, and liabilities, does not automatically transfer to heirs. Instead, it may need to go through a court-supervised process called **probate**, which ensures debts are paid and assets are distributed properly. Whether probate is required depends on several factors, including the value of the estate, the presence of a will, and whether assets are structured to avoid probate.

In California, if the total gross value of a decedent's estate is $166,250 or less (as of January 1, 2025), it may qualify for simplified procedures such as the *Small Estate Affidavit,* under California Probate Code § 13100. This process allows heirs to transfer certain assets without going through formal probate, provided at least 40 days have passed since the date of death and no formal probate has been initiated. However, estates that exceed this threshold, particularly those involving real estate, individually owned financial accounts, or assets without designated **beneficiaries**, individuals designated to receive

1

specific assets, generally require full probate unless the assets were held in a revocable living trust or another probate-avoidance structure. A trust is a legal arrangement in which a person (the grantor) places assets under the management of a **trustee**, a person or entity who holds and distributes the property according to the terms of the trust, for the benefit of named beneficiaries.

Probate can be straightforward when there are no disputes, but it can quickly become a complex legal battle when disagreements arise over the validity of a trust or will, the handling of assets, or the executor's actions. Whether you are an executor, a beneficiary, or someone contesting a will, understanding probate is crucial. In this chapter, you'll get a clear overview of probate: what it is, when it's required, how the process works, and why some cases become courtroom battles.

What is Probate?

Probate is the legal process of administering a deceased person's estate (California Probate Code §§ 8200, 13050, 2025). It ensures that all debts, taxes, and financial obligations are settled before assets are distributed to heirs or beneficiaries.

If the deceased left a valid will, probate involves validating the will's authenticity and ensuring that the **executor**, the person named in the will to manage the estate, carries out the deceased's wishes under court supervision. If there is no will, probate follows *state intestacy laws*, which dictate how assets are divided among surviving relatives (*California Probate Code §§ 6400 et seq.*, 2024).

For example, intestacy laws in California state that if both parents are deceased and there is no surviving spouse, the estate is divided equally among all living biological children. If a biological child has also passed away, their share of the estate would be inherited by their children (the deceased's grandchildren) in equal portions. If there are no direct descendants, the estate may be distributed to siblings of the deceased, nieces, nephews, or more distant relatives, depending on state law.

Not all estates require probate. Some assets pass automatically to heirs without court involvement, such as jointly owned property with right of survivorship, payable-on-death (POD) bank accounts, life insurance policies with named beneficiaries, and assets placed in a revocable living trust. However, disputes over a will, trust, or estate administration can still lead to probate litigation.

Wills vs. Trusts: What's the Difference?

A will and a living trust are both legal tools that allow a person to decide what happens to their assets after they pass away. However, they work in very different ways, and understanding these differences is key to knowing how probate applies to an estate (see Table 1.1, *Wills vs. Trusts*).

A *will* is a legal document that states how a person's assets should be distributed after their death. It also allows them to name an executor, the person responsible for carrying out those instructions. If minor children are involved, a will can also designate a legal guardian.

However, a will does not avoid probate. When a person dies with a will, their estate must still go through the court-supervised probate process before assets can be distributed. This can result in delays, court costs, and potential disputes. Additionally, once a will is filed with the court, it becomes public record, meaning anyone can access its contents.

A *living trust*, on the other hand, is a legal arrangement where a person places assets into a trust while they are still alive. The person who creates the trust, known as the **grantor** (or settlor), also serves as the trustee, maintaining full control over their assets during their lifetime. Most living trusts are revocable, meaning the grantor can modify or dissolve them at any time. If the grantor becomes incapacitated due to conditions like dementia or Alzheimer's, the successor trustee typically steps in to manage the trust on the grantor's behalf. Upon the grantor's death, the trust becomes irrevocable, and no further changes can be made. At this point, the grantor is legally referred to as the decedent. The successor trustee, or simply trustee if they had already assumed the role due to incapacity, continues managing the trust. They are legally required to act in the best interest of the beneficiaries and follow the instructions outlined in the trust document.

If the decedent had only a will instead of a trust, the estate would typically go through probate, and an executor (not a trustee) would be appointed to manage the distribution of assets. Unlike a will, which takes effect only after death, a trust also allows for financial management during the grantor's lifetime, including periods of incapacity.

A living trust that has been *properly funded*, meaning the grantor transferred their assets into the trust during their lifetime, can bypass probate entirely. This allows **heirs**, those entitled to inherit assets from the decedent, to receive their inheritance more quickly and privately. Since the court is not involved, trust assets remain private and do not become part of the public record. However, before any assets are distributed, all debts, taxes, and expenses must be paid. If the successor trustee fails to notify creditors properly, they may be held personally liable for unpaid debts.

As shown in Table 1.1, the choice between a will and a trust has significant implications for probate, privacy, and control during one's lifetime.

A *pour-over will* works in combination with a trust to catch any assets that were not properly transferred. These assets transferred through a pour-over will must still go through probate before entering the trust.

Table 1.1. Wills vs. Trusts

Category	Wills	Trusts
Takes effect	After death	Immediately
Court involvement	Required (goes through probate)	Avoids probate if properly funded
Privacy	Public record	Private documents
Incapacity protection	None	Successor trustee takes over
Changes allowed	Yes (until death if competent)	Yes, if revocable; no, if irrevocable
Asset manager	Court-appointed executor	Trustee or successor trustee
Main purpose	Distributes assets after death	Manage assets during life and after death

Note. This table summarizes the major differences between a will and a living trust, including how each affects probate, privacy, control, and incapacity planning.

Many people also misunderstand what wills and trusts actually do. See Table 1.2, *Common Misconceptions about Wills vs. Trusts*, for a breakdown of two common myths and the truth behind them.

Table 1.2. Common Misconceptions About Wills vs. Trusts

Misconception	Truth
"If I have a will, I can avoid probate."	Wills go through probate
"Trusts can't be contested."	They can—through trust litigation

Note. Many people misunderstand how wills and trusts actually work. This table highlights two of the most common misconceptions—both of which can lead to serious mistakes when planning an estate or deciding whether to contest one

Understanding the Differences Between Probate and Trust Administration

Although both probate and trust administration aim to settle a person's estate, they involve distinct processes, responsibilities, and degrees of court supervision. Probate typically requires formal court involvement, including filing a **petition** (a formal written request to the court), notifying heirs and creditors, and obtaining court approval for asset distribution. In contrast, trust administration usually operates without routine court oversight, focusing instead on the trustee managing and distributing assets according to the trust's terms.

One key difference is who takes charge: In probate, the executor (or **administrator** if no will exists, someone appointed by the court to manage the estate) is responsible, while in trust administration, the trustee or successor trustee oversees the process. Additionally, probate cases often involve court-supervised appraisals, while trustees independently manage asset valuation.

From a legal standpoint, disputes in probate are handled as probate litigation, whereas trust disputes fall under trust litigation. Additionally, the duration and costs of probate can be significantly higher due to statutory fees based on estate value, while trustee fees vary and are often negotiable.

See Table 1.3, *Probate vs. Trust Administration: Key Differences* for a concise comparison of these two processes.

Table 1.3. Probate vs. Trust Administration: Key Differences

Topic	Probate	Trust Administration
Court involvement	Required unless simplified procedure applies	Not required unless disputed
Legal process name	Probate	Trust Administration
Responsible party	Executor (or Administrator if no will)	Trustee (or Successor Trustee if unable to serve)
Governing document	Will (or intestacy law if no will)	Trust Document
What disputes are called	Probate Litigation	Trust Litigation
Common code sections	Probate Code §§ 8000-10592 (estate administration)	Probate Code § 17200 (trust disputes)

Note. Probate and trust administration are both handled by the probate division of the superior court in California. While trusts are designed to avoid probate, disputes can still trigger court involvement through a trust petition. Executors and trustees share fiduciary responsibilities, but the procedures and oversight differ significantly.

Procedural Differences Between Probate and Trust Administration

The probate process is typically court-supervised, involving formal hearings, judicial approvals, and mandatory public filings. It requires filing a petition with the court and providing notice to heirs and creditors. In contrast, trust administration is generally handled outside of court, focusing primarily on notifying beneficiaries and often avoiding public filings altogether. In probate, an inventory and appraisal of estate assets are conducted by a court-appointed referee, while in trust administration, the trustee handles these tasks independently. Probate involves statutory fees based on the total value of the estate, whereas trustee fees are typically calculated based on the trust agreement or are subject to the trustee's reasonable compensation, but are not fixed by statute. Probate proceedings often take months or even years to complete, while trust administration generally moves more quickly unless a dispute arises (see Table 1.4, *Procedural Differences Between Probate and Trust Administration*).

Table 1.4. Procedural Differences Between Probate and Trust Administration

Topic	Probate	Trust Administration
Court Supervision	Mandatory, with hearings and approvals	Typically private; court involvement if contested
Filing and Notice	Petition, public notice, and notifications to heirs and creditors	Notice mainly to beneficiaries; no public filing
Inventory and Appraisal	Required, with court-appointed referee	Handled by trustee without court involvement
Court Fees	Statutory fees based on estate value	Trustee fees vary and are not statutory
Duration	Several months to years	Generally faster, unless contested

Note. This table highlights key procedural differences between probate and trust administration, including court oversight, notice, appraisal, fees, and duration. Understanding these distinctions clarifies the legal steps required in each process.

When is Probate Necessary?

Whether probate is required depends on how assets were titled at the time of death. Probate is typically required when assets are solely in the decedent's name, meaning they are not jointly owned, do not have a named beneficiary, and are not held in a trust (California Probate Code § 13050, 2024). Figure 1.1 illustrates which types of assets typically require probate and which do not (see Figure 1.1, *Assets that Bypass Probate*). For example, if a real estate property was titled only in the decedent's name and was not placed in a trust, it must go through probate before it can be transferred to heirs. Similarly, bank accounts without a designated payable-on-death (POD) or transfer-on-death (TOD) beneficiary require probate before funds can be accessed. Personal property, such as vehicles, jewelry, or household items, must also go through probate unless the estate qualifies for a small estate affidavit or a similar state exemption. Investment and retirement accounts that do not have a named beneficiary, or where the named beneficiary has passed away, may also require probate before distribution.

Certain assets bypass probate entirely when they are properly designated. Real estate that is owned as joint tenants with right of survivorship (JTWROS) or by a married couple as community property with right of survivorship automatically transfers to the surviving owner without probate. Bank accounts, investment accounts, and retirement funds that have a POD or TOD designation go directly to the named beneficiary. Life insurance proceeds also pass directly to the designated beneficiary without court involvement. Additionally, assets that were properly transferred into a revocable living trust before the decedent's death can be distributed according to the trust's terms without needing to go through probate.

- Jointly owned property with rights of survivorship, such as a home owned by a married couple.
- Payable-on-death (POD) and transfer-on-death (TOD) accounts, including bank and investment accounts.
- Life insurance policies, retirement accounts (IRAs, 401(k)s), and annuities with named beneficiaries.
- Assets held in a properly funded revocable living trust.

Figure 1.1. Assets That Bypass Probate
Probate is required for assets titled solely in the decedent's name without a beneficiary or trust designation. However, some assets transfer outside of probate when they are jointly owned or have a named beneficiary.

Keep in mind . . . even if an estate is structured to avoid probate, legal challenges can still trigger court involvement. Disputes over the validity of the will, claims of undue influence, or disagreements among beneficiaries may lead to litigation, requiring court oversight. Additionally, if a person fails to transfer trust assets into a trust or forgets to update beneficiary designations, those assets may still need to go through probate.

The need for probate depends on state laws, the structure of the estate, and whether any legal challenges arise. Understanding these factors can help individuals plan effectively to minimize costs, and complications for their heirs.

California Probate Thresholds for Small Estates

In California, estates valued under $184,500 (as of 2023) do not require full probate and may qualify for a simplified process under California Probate Code § 13100 (2025). Instead of formal probate, heirs can use a *Small Estate Affidavit* to transfer assets without court involvement. However, this $184,500 probate threshold applies only to assets subject to probate. Assets that already have a designated beneficiary, are held in a trust, or are jointly owned with survivorship rights do not count toward this limit because they transfer automatically outside of probate.

For small estates, probate is not required if the total value is below $184,500. However, if the estate includes real property worth more than $62,500, a simplified court procedure may still be necessary. If an estate exceeds these limits, it will likely require formal probate unless the assets were properly structured to avoid it (California Probate Code §§ 13100, 13200, 2025).

Overview of the Probate Process

The probate process begins when someone (typically the person named in the will as executor or a close family member) files a *petition for probate* with the court. This petition requests that the court open a probate case and appoint someone to manage the estate. Probate is only required when assets are not held in a living trust. If the deceased had a will, the court will validate it and formally appoint the named executor. If there is no will, the court appoints an administrator, and the estate is distributed according to *California's intestate succession laws*.

Once appointed, the executor or administrator must notify all **interested parties**, individuals or entities who have a legal right or claim to be involved In the probate proceedings, including heirs and known creditors. This includes mailing notices to known individuals and publishing a Notice of Petition to Administer Estate in a court-approved newspaper to alert unknown creditors and other interested parties. They must also prepare an inventory of the estate's assets. Debts and taxes must be paid before any assets can be distributed. Creditors are given a limited time to file claims, and the estate must cover all outstanding obligations, including final income taxes and any estate taxes owed.

After settling debts, the executor distributes the remaining assets according to the terms of the will, or according to state law if no will exists. Finally, the executor files a *petition for final distribution*, asking the court to approve the proposed distributions and officially close the estate.

Key Players in Probate

Several individuals and entities play essential roles in the probate process (see Table 1.5, *Key Players in the Probate Process*). The **executor**, named in the will, is responsible for overseeing the estate's administration, ensuring debts are paid, and distributing assets according to the deceased's wishes. If there is no will, the court appoints an **administrator**, who functions similarly to an executor but follows the state's intestacy laws.

The **probate judge** oversees the process and ensures that the executor or administrator complies with legal requirements.

Beneficiaries and heirs are those who will inherit assets, either through the will or under state law. Additionally, **creditors**, including banks, mortgage lenders, and tax agencies, must be notified, as they have the right to claim outstanding debts before any inheritance is distributed.

If disputes arise between heirs, creditors, or the executor, **probate litigation** may become necessary. This can prolong the process and increase legal costs.

Table 1.5. Key Players in the Probate Process

Role	Description
Executor	Named in the will to carry out the decedent's instructions and manage the estate.
Administrator	Appointed by the court if no will exists. Performs similar duties under intestate laws.
Trustee	Manages a living trust; the successor trustee takes over if the grantor is deceased or incapacitated.
Beneficiaries	Individuals or entities named in the will or trust to receive assets.
Heirs	Individuals entitled to inherit under state law if there is no valid will.
Probate Judge	Oversees probate, resolves disputes, and approves distributions.
Creditors	Owed money by the decedent. Must be notified and can file claims.
Attorneys	Represents parties such as executors, trustees, beneficiaries in trust disputes.

Note. Not every probate case involves all these players. If no will exists, there will be no executor—only an administrator. In trust cases, the trustee plays the lead role rather than an executor.

Why Wills and Trusts Get Contested

While many probate and trust administrations proceed without conflict, disputes can arise, turning what should be a straightforward process into a legal battle. These legal battles can fall under *probate* litigation or *trust litigation*, depending on whether a will or a trust in involved. Both types of cases are handled in probate court.

The most common reason probate becomes contested is when someone challenges the validity of a will, often claiming undue influence, fraud, or lack of capacity when the will was created. Disputes can also occur if an executor is accused of mismanaging the estate, failing to act in the best interests of the beneficiaries, or engaging in financial misconduct.

However, living trusts, which are designed to avoid probate, can still be challenged in probate court. If someone believes the trust was created under suspicious circumstances or that the trustee is failing in their duties, they may file a *trust petition* in probate court. These cases fall under *trust litigation*, often filed under *Probate Code § 17200*, and may involve allegations like undue influence, lack of capacity, or breach of fiduciary duty.

Disagreements are especially common in blended families, second marriages, or when long-lost or estranged relatives are involved. Whether the issue involves a will or a trust, unresolved disputes can lead to full litigation, including court hearings, discovery, motions, and even trial.

Conclusion

Probate is an essential legal process that ensures a deceased person's estate is handled correctly, but it can be complex and, in some cases, highly contentious. While many probate cases follow a straightforward path, disputes over wills, executors, and asset distribution can lead to drawn-out litigation. And even when probate is avoided through a living trust, legal challenges may still arise, often leading to trust litigation in probate court.

Understanding the basic probate process, and how it differs from trust administration, will help prepare you for the legal journey ahead.

In the next chapter, we'll explore the steps involved in a contested probate case, from filing petitions to preparing for trial.

Figure 1.2 highlights the key takeaways from this chapter to reinforce your understanding.

1. Probate is a court-supervised process for distributing a deceased person's assets, paying debts, and settling the estate. It is typically required when assets are titled solely in the decedent's name and are not structured to avoid probate.
2. **Wills vs. Trusts:** A will outlines who inherits what and names an executor but does not avoid probate. A properly funded living trust bypasses probate, keeping assets private and accessible.
3. **Small Estates:** In California, estates valued under $184,500 (as of 2023) may avoid full probate through simplified procedures, like a Small Estate Affidavit. However, real property over $62,500 may still require probate.
4. **Probate Disputes:** Common disputes include challenges to wills or trusts, claims of executor misconduct, or conflicts among beneficiaries. Both will and trust disputes are resolved in probate court.
5. **Key Players:** The process involves the executor or administrator, beneficiaries, creditors, and the probate judge. If contested, litigation can increase the cost and extend the timeline.
6. **Why This Matters:** Understanding probate helps you anticipate delays, avoid mistakes, and prepare for what lies ahead—especially if you're representing yourself.

Figure 1.2. Key Takeaways – Understanding Probate
This figure highlights the key points of Chapter 1, covering the probate process, when it is required, and the differences between wills and living trusts.

CHAPTER 2

Steps Toward Trial: A Brief Roadmap

Introduction

This chapter provides a roadmap to help you understand the typical steps from filing a petition to reaching trial, or settling beforehand. Some cases resolve quickly, while others move through multiple stages, each with its own challenges.

The flowchart (see Figure 2.1, *Key Steps in a Probate Dispute*) below gives a big-picture view of how a contested probate case might unfold. While each case is unique, many follow a similar sequence of events:

After the opposing party responds, litigation may proceed to Discovery, where both sides gather evidence. At a later court hearing, the judge may order a Mandatory Settlement Conference (MSC) to encourage resolution. (Note: Not all states or counties require an MSC, but many courts use them to reduce the number of cases that go to trial.) If disputes remain unresolved, Pre-Trial Motions may follow. These are formal requests asking the judge to decide legal issues before trial begins. For example, a party might file a motion to exclude evidence or a motion for summary judgment, arguing that the case should be dismissed without going to trial.

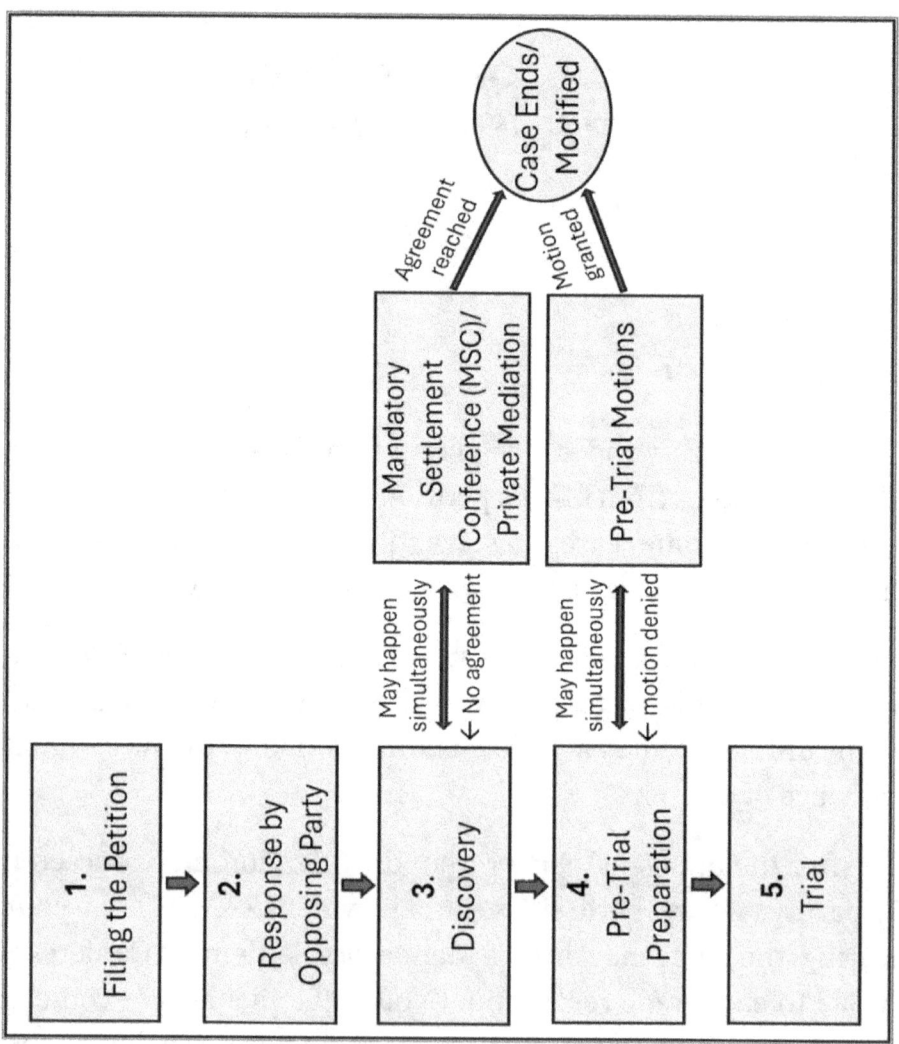

Figure 2.1. Key Steps in a Probate Dispute
A simplified overview of key stages in a contested probate or trust case, including optional steps like MSC and pre-trial motions.

In the sections that follow, we'll briefly explain what happens at each stage.

Understanding this roadmap can help you feel more prepared and less overwhelmed as your case moves forward.

The Steps to a Contested Probate Case: From Filing to Trial

Contested probate cases often follow a structured path, from the initial petition to the discovery phase and beyond. Understanding these key steps will help you navigate the process effectively and anticipate what comes next.

What Triggers a Petition? Why Legal Action Begins in Trust and Will Cases

Before a probate or trust case can move forward in court, someone has to file a petition. But what leads someone to file? Whether the dispute involves a *will* (which triggers probate litigation) or a *living trust* (which falls under trust litigation), there's usually a triggering event that prompts legal action. It may involve concerns about the validity of a document, the conduct of a fiduciary, or the mishandling of assets.

While both types of litigation deal with a decedent's assets, the process for initiating court involvement, and the reasons for doing so, can differ depending on whether you are dealing with a will or a trust.

SELF-REPRESENTED

In **probate cases**, which usually involves a will, the person named as executor in the will has a legal duty to take certain steps after the decedent's death. First, they are required to lodge the original will with the court, usually within 30 days. They are also expected to file a petition to open probate and request appointment as executor. Once the court sets a hearing, it is their responsibility to serve formal notice (called the Notice of Petition to Administer Estate) on all interested parties, including heirs and named beneficiaries. If the named executor fails to take these steps, either by doing nothing or by attempting to manage assets without court approval, any interested person can step in and file a petition. This might include a request to admit the will, to be appointed administrator, or to contest the validity of the will entirely.

In **trust litigation**, which usually involves a living trust, court involvement typically begins after the death of the settlor (the person who created the trust). At that point, the trust usually becomes irrevocable, and the trustee is responsible for administering it. Unlike wills, trusts do not go through probate automatically, which means the trustee may begin managing or distributing assets without any court oversight. However, under *California Probate Code § 16061.7*, the trustee is legally required to send a **Notice of Trust Administration**, a formal notification informing heirs and beneficiaries that the trust is being administered to all heirs and beneficiaries. This notice starts a limited time window (usually 120 days) for someone to contest the trust or a recent amendment.

Litigation begins only when someone files a petition to bring the matter into court, often under Probate Code § 17200.

Common legal grounds include allegations that the trust or a late amendment is invalid due to undue influence, fraud, or lack of capacity. A petition may also be filed if the trustee fails to provide an accounting, withholds financial records, delays distributions, or breaches their fiduciary duties. Sometimes beneficiaries are excluded entirely or receive unequal treatment, and a petition may be the only way to challenge the terms of the trust or compel the trustee to act properly.

In many cases, nothing is filed right away after someone dies—not a will, not a trust notice, not a petition. This can happen because the family is overwhelmed, unsure what to do, or because the person in charge decides to handle everything informally. But if there are significant assets involved, or if someone has been left out or kept in the dark, this silence can raise concerns.

If you are a beneficiary, heir, or creditor and you haven't received any notice, you may want to check with the probate court to see if anything has been filed. If not, you can take legal action yourself. You may be able to petition the court to open probate, admit the will, or appoint a new administrator. In trust cases, you can file a petition to bring the matter before a judge and request information or challenge the trustee's actions. In both scenarios, the court will not act unless someone takes the first step.

Wondering If Anything Should be Filed

If a loved one has died and you haven't received any legal documents—no court petition, no trust notice, no official accounting—it's okay to ask questions. Whether there's a will, a trust, or no documents at all, something should usually be filed with the court.

- ❖ If there's a will, someone should petition the court to admit it and open probate.
- ❖ If there's a living trust, the trustee should send out a formal Notice of Administration.
- ❖ If the estate is small (under $184,500 in California), a small estate affidavit may be used instead of full probate.

The Steps to Trial

Step 1: Filing the Petition

A contested probate case begins when someone files a formal petition in probate court. This petition may challenge the validity of a will or trust or raise concerns about how the estate or trust is being managed. Common legal claims include undue influence, fraud, or lack of capacity—especially if a will or trust amendment appears suspicious. In some cases, the **petitioner**, the person who files the petition, may be objecting to the appointment of an executor or trustee, often citing a conflict of interest or evidence that the person is unfit to serve. Others may be challenging how the estate or trust is being handled, pointing to mismanagement of assets, delays in distribution, or failure to act in the best interests of the beneficiaries.

To initiate the case, the petitioner must file a legal petition that clearly states the claims being made and the relief being sought. This may include requests to invalidate a document, compel an accounting, remove a fiduciary, or appoint someone else to manage the estate. The petition should be supported by any relevant evidence, such as financial records, communications, or medical documentation. Along with the petition, the filer must submit the required court forms and pay the **filing fee** (the amount paid to officially submit a document to court). Once accepted by the court, the case officially begins, and notice must be served on all interested parties.

Step 2: Responding to the Petition

Once the petition is filed, the opposing party, often the executor, trustee, or a beneficiary, has the right to respond. They may deny the claims, file a counter-petition or legal motions, and submit their own evidence. In some cases, instead of simply objecting, the opposing party may file a Motion to Dismiss, asking the court to throw out the case before it proceeds. If the court grants the motion, the case ends immediately. If the court denies it, the case moves to the next phase: Discovery.

Step 3: Discovery – Gathering Evidence

If the case moves forward, both sides collect and exchange evidence in a process known as Discovery. This phase allows parties to request and obtain information relevant to their claims and defenses, helping them build their case before trial.

Evidence collection methods include Requests for Admissions (*California Code of Civil Procedure § 2033.010*), where a party formally asks the other side to admit or deny specific facts, and Form Interrogatories (*California Code of Civil Procedure § 2030.010*), which require written responses under oath. These two discovery tools are often served simultaneously to clarify key facts and narrow the issues before trial.

A Request for the Production of Documents (*California Code of Civil Procedure § 2031.010*) is used to obtain financial records, emails, medical reports, or other relevant materials. Subpoenas (*California Code of Civil Procedure § 1985*) may be issued to legally compel third parties to provide testimony or produce documents. Attorneys may also conduct depositions (*California Code of Civil Procedure § 2025.010*), where witnesses provide sworn testimony before trial. In some cases, parties may submit *sworn affidavits*, which are written statements made under oath that may serve as evidence.

While Discovery allows parties to obtain evidence, the admissibility of that evidence at trial is determined later by the judge through **motions** (formal requests for court orders), **objections** (challenges to the admissibility of evidence or other procedural or legal issues), and **evidentiary rulings** (judicial decisions presented in court).

Because Discovery can be complex and often involves large volumes of documents, a more detailed breakdown will be provided in a future volume of this guide."

Settlement Options: MSC and Private Mediation

At some point before trial, the court may require both parties to attend a **Mandatory Settlement Conference (MSC)**, a court-ordered meeting where parties attempt to resolve their dispute with the assistance of a neutral judge or settlement officer. Governed by *California Rules of Court, Rule 3.1380* or by local probate rules, the MSC is a formal opportunity for both sides to negotiate a resolution with the assistance of a neutral judge or court-appointed settlement officer. MSCs are free and often scheduled by the court during or after the Discovery phase. Many cases settle at this stage, avoiding the time and expense of trial.

In addition to MSCs, parties may also choose to participate in **private mediation** at any point in the case—whether before, during, or even after Discovery. Private mediation is voluntary and typically involves hiring a professional mediator, often a retired judge or experienced probate attorney to facilitate settlement discussions. While private mediation can offer more flexibility, privacy, and time for negotiation, it also comes with a cost, which may range from several thousand dollars up to $10,000 or more depending on the complexity of the case and the mediator's hourly rate.

Whether through a court-ordered MSC or private mediation, settlement is always possible, and often encouraged, to avoid the risks and emotional toll of trial.

Step 4: Pre-Trial Preparation and Settlement Efforts

Once Discovery is complete, both parties begin preparing for trial. This phase involves organizing evidence, preparing witnesses, and finalizing legal arguments. Unlike the earlier stages of the case where much of the work takes place between the parties, pre-trial preparation requires direct court involvement. Exhibits must be marked (assigned an exhibit number), labeled, and submitted to the court according to **local rules**, specific procedural guidelines by each court that dictate how documents must be filed, labeled, and presented. Parties may also need to file witness lists, exhibit lists, and pre-trial briefs, all by strict deadlines.

Even at this stage, settlement is still possible. While a Mandatory Settlement Conference (MSC) may have already occurred during Discovery, some courts may allow or encourage further settlement efforts before trial. In other cases, the parties may choose to pursue *private mediation,* a voluntary process facilitated by a neutral professional—often a retired judge or probate attorney. Private mediation offers greater flexibility and confidentiality but can come at a significant cost, often ranging from several thousand dollars to as much as $10,000. Whether through court-sponsored or private efforts, late-stage settlement remains a valuable option before trial begins.

Pre-Trial Motions: Shaping the Case Before Trial

Pre-trial motions are legal tools that allow either party to ask the judge to make rulings before trial begins. These motions may help narrow the issues, clarify what evidence will be allowed, or even end the case entirely.

One of the most powerful pre-trial tools is the **Motion for Summary Judgment**, where a party argues that the facts are undisputed, and the law is clearly in their favor. If the court agrees, it can rule without trial. If the motion is denied, the case continues to trial as planned.

Another common motion is a **Motion in Limine**, which asks the judge to exclude certain evidence from being introduced at trial. These motions rely on the *rules of evidence* that typically argue that the material is irrelevant, hearsay, unduly prejudicial, or otherwise inadmissible under the California Evidence Code.

In some cases, a party may also file a **Motion to Compel Discovery** if the opposing side failed to turn over documents or answer questions during the Discovery phase. These are typically heard before trial begins, and if granted, the court can order the release of the missing information.

Pre-trial motions can significantly affect the course of litigation. They may result in a full or partial dismissal of claims, limit what can be presented at trial, or shift the balance of power between the parties. Even in cases that proceed to trial, these motions often define what the judge will hear and what they won't.

Bench vs. Jury Trial:
What to Expect in Probate Cases

- In a **bench trial**, the judge decides both the law and the facts. This is the standard format for probate and trust litigation—meaning the judge alone reviews the evidence, applies the law, and issues a ruling.
- In contrast, a **jury trial** involves a group of citizens (the jury) who listen to the evidence and decide the facts of the case, while the judge handles legal rulings. Jury trials are common in criminal and general civil cases but are rare in probate court.

In limited probate matters—like will contests—a jury trial can sometimes be requested. However, this requires special procedures and may involve additional costs. Unless the court grants your jury request, assume your case will be heard by a judge.

Step 5: Trial – The Final Decision

If the case hasn't settled or been dismissed, it moves forward to trial. Most probate trials are bench trials, which means they are heard by a judge and not a jury. The judge listens to all the evidence, makes rulings on what's admissible, and ultimately decides the outcome of the case.

The trial follows a structured sequence, typically including the following stages (see Table 2.1, *Trial Stages*).

Table 2.1. Trial Stages

Stage	What Happens
1. Opening Statements	Each side gives a brief overview of their case and what they intend to prove, starting with the petitioner.
2. Present Evidence	The petitioner begins by calling witnesses, followed by cross-examination from the opposing side. Then the respondent presents their case with the petitioner then cross-examining.
3. Rebuttal (if allowed)	The petitioner may offer new evidence or arguments in response to the respondent's case, if permitted by the court.
4. Closing Arguments	Each side summarizes their case. The petitioner goes first, followed by the respondent. Sometimes the petitioner gets a brief final rebuttal.
5. Judge's Decision	The judge may issue a ruling immediately or take the matter "under submission" and issue a written ruling later.

Note: Most probate trials are bench trials, meaning the judge hears the evidence and makes the final decision. In rare cases, a jury may be permitted.

After the trial begins with opening statements, the petitioner presents their case first, followed by the **respondent**, the person or party opposing the petition. Both sides may call witnesses, introduce documents, and cross-examine opposing witnesses. If allowed, the petitioner may present a brief rebuttal to address new evidence introduced by the respondent.

The trial concludes with closing arguments. The petitioner goes first, summarizing their case, followed by the respondent. Sometimes, the petitioner may be given a brief word. After the closing arguments, the judge may issue an immediate decision or take the case under submission, issuing a written ruling later.

For pro pers, trial preparation can feel overwhelming. It's not just about telling your story. It's about presenting facts and evidence in a structured way that matches your legal claims. Even if you're representing yourself, you must follow the same basic rules of evidence and procedure. The judge may be patient, but you're still expected to present your case clearly and efficiently.

To understand what this process looks like in real life, let's look at one actual case that never made it to trial, but still tested every step of the system.

Behind the Case — A Real-Life Probate Battle

When people ask how long a contested probate case can take, the only honest answer is: *It depends.*

In our own case, it took over two and a half years—even though we never reached trial. What follows is a timeline and narrative that illustrates how complicated, drawn-out, and emotionally taxing probate litigation can be, even when settlement is eventually reached.

If the timeline looks complicated or hard to follow—that's intentional. It reflects just how overwhelming and confusing the process can be in real time, especially when you're navigating it without an attorney. That complexity is part of the lived reality of contested probate.

Figure 2.2 shows a timeline that reflects just how much can unfold *before* trial, even in a case that never makes it to the courtroom (see Figure 2.2, *Timeline of Probate Filings and Court Appearances (2022-2025)*).

SELF-REPRESENTED

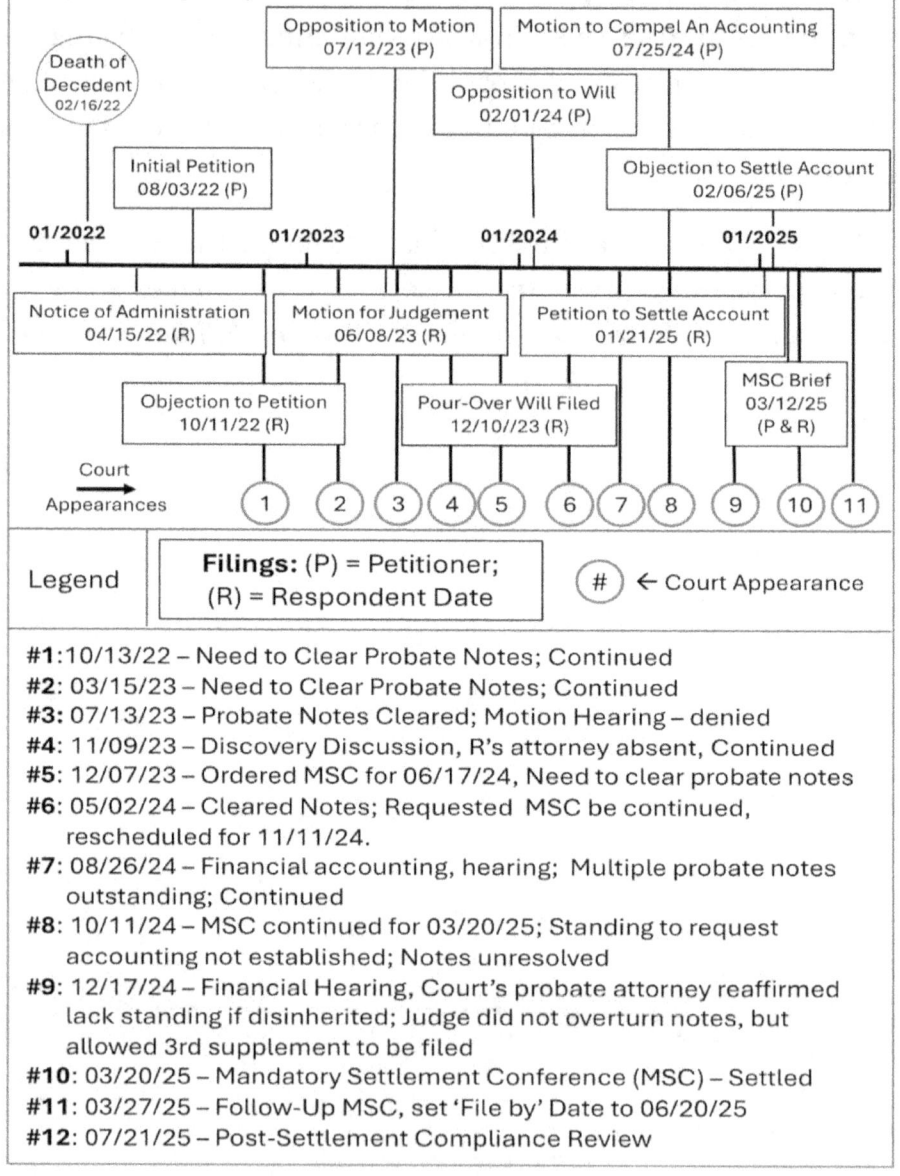

Figure 2.2. Timeline of Filings and Court Appearances
Major probate filings and court appearances from 2022 to 2025, illustrating the procedural complexity and duration of a contested case that did not reach trial.

When people ask how long a contested probate case can take, I can only answer with two words: It depends.

In my own experience, the process took over two and a half years, even without going to trial.

We filed our initial petition in August 2022 to contest a trust that disinherited six of seven siblings. Over the next 31 months, our case involved multiple filings, court hearings, and repeated delays due to unresolved **probate notes**, court-issued comments or questions about the petition that must be addressed before the case can proceed. We entered the discovery phase without a financial accounting and were ordered to attend a Mandatory Settlement Conference (MSC) without the key documents we had requested. Despite asking for continuances, we were told the next available MSC would not be until 2026 due to court backlogs. So, we moved forward.

We eventually settled at the third scheduled MSC in March 2025, while still in discovery and preparing for pre-trial motions. Although we never made it to trial, we spent years gathering evidence, filing objections, and responding to counter-petitions. Our case included a petition to invalidate the trust, an objection to a newly filed pour-over will, a motion to compel a financial accounting, and an objection to the respondent's petition to settle an account. The court eventually consolidated related matters into a single case.

Nearly every court hearing was continued to allow time to "clear the notes," a process that required supplemental filings and constant follow-up. Discovery was slow and often incomplete. There were arguments over standing, debates about relevant case law, and disputes about whether we were even entitled to a financial accounting.

And through it all, we pressed on.

This timeline is not unusual. Contested probate cases can stretch out for years due to legal complexity, lack of cooperation, and delays in the court system. Even without a trial, the process can be exhausting. But the public docket only tells part of the story. What isn't captured are the late nights, unpaid hours, and quiet sacrifices that come with representing yourself in a contested probate matter.

In this guide, I'll Walk you through how to file your initial petition, just like the one we filed at the beginning of this long journey. Later volumes will cover discovery, gathering evidence, and preparing for trial. For now, just know this: you are not alone, and you can do this.

A Note From the Author:
The Hidden Hours

I spent over 400 hours on this case. Probably more.

That includes filing petitions, responding to objections, writing supplements, and navigating the never-ending demands of discovery. But it doesn't include the hours I spent off the clock—listening to probate podcasts, watching YouTube videos, jumping on webinars to ask questions, or going on long runs just trying to figure things out.

I wasn't trained in law. I learned by doing—because I had to. And through that process, I became the person who knew the case better than anyone. Every timeline, every filing, every contradiction—I held it all in my head. I didn't need to relearn it each time I opened the file like a paid lawyer would.

Most of that time was spent researching, making mistakes, and asking questions until I figured it out. And while I can't take the emotional weight off your shoulders, I created this guide so that you don't have to spend hundreds of hours just getting started. I did the hard work, so you don't have to.

Self-representation isn't just advocacy. It's being your own paralegal, legal researcher, strategist, and case manager. And while that may feel overwhelming, it can also be your greatest strength—because no one will ever care about your case the way you do.

These are the hidden hours behind every page of a court file. Now, let's recap what really matters as you prepare for your own case.

Conclusion

Not all cases go to trial. Many end early through private mediation, summary judgment, or a motion to dismiss. The opposing party can attempt to end the case early by filing a Motion to Dismiss. If the case survives dismissal, the discovery phase becomes critical, as the strength of the evidence often determines the likelihood of settlement or success at trial.

Even after discovery, there are multiple opportunities to resolve the case before trial, including Mandatory Settlement Conferences (MSC) and pre-trial motions. Every step of the process requires careful preparation. Missed deadlines, disorganized exhibits, or unsupported claims can weaken your position or result in the case being dismissed.

Finally, it's important to understand that contested probate cases often take years to resolve. Legal motions, continuances, discovery disputes, and trial scheduling can significantly extend the timeline. Patience, organization, and persistence are essential for navigating the road to resolution whether your case ends in settlement or trial.

Stay focused on your purpose, prepare each step with care, and know that every filing, deadline, and decision brings you closer to clarity, and, hopefully, justice.

To wrap up this chapter, Figure 2.3 outlines the key takeaways of the main steps and concepts involved in navigating contested probate cases (see Figure 2.3, *Key Takeaways – Steps Toward Trial*).

> Contested probate cases generally follow these stages:
> 1. **Filing the Petition:** The petitioner files a legal petition, outlining the claims, legal grounds, and requested relief. This formally initiates court involvement.
> 2. **Response to the Petition:** The opposing party may file an objection, submit counterclaims, or request dismissal of the petition.
> 3. **Discovery:** Both sides collect and exchange evidence, such as documents, witness statements, and expert testimony. Discovery often shapes the strength and strategy of each case before trial.
> 4. **Settlement Opportunities:** Mandatory Settlement Conferences (MSC) and private mediation provide opportunities to resolve the dispute without going to trial.
> 5. **Pre-Trial Motions:** Parties may file motions to dismiss, exclude evidence, or narrow the issues. These motions can significantly shape the trial—or even end the case entirely.
> 6. **Trial:** If no settlement is reached, the case goes to trial—typically a bench trial in probate court. The judge hears testimony, reviews evidence, assesses credibility, and issues a ruling.
> 7. **Post-Trial Considerations:** After trial, parties may file motions to modify or reconsider the ruling, or appeal the decision to a higher court.

Figure 2.3. Key Takeaways – Steps Toward Trial
Highlights major phases of a contested probate case—from filing to trial—and emphasizes the role of preparation, discovery, and early settlement efforts to resolve disputes effectively.

PART II

Before Filing a Petition

Filing a petition to challenge a trust or will is a serious legal action that requires careful preparation. This section covers critical pre-filing considerations, including probate deadlines and whether you have legal standing to file. Ensuring you meet eligibility requirements and deadlines will prevent unnecessary delays or dismissals.

CHAPTER 3

Understanding Deadlines

Introduction

Meeting deadlines is crucial when contesting a trust, will, or fiduciary misconduct in California probate cases. Missing a deadline can result in permanently losing your right to challenge the matter. California has strict rules about when and how to file, so it's essential to understand these deadlines before taking any action.

This chapter breaks down the key deadlines you need to know, including the **120-day Rule** for trust contests, the timeline for will objections, and how to address cases of fraud or breach of fiduciary duty. The 120-Day Rule refers to the legal deadline under *California Probate Code § 16061.8*, which gives you 120 days from the date you're served with a Notice of Trust Administration to file a petition contesting a living trust. You'll also learn what to do if your petition is rejected and how to correct mistakes while preserving your rights.

Understanding the 120-Day Filing Rule

Under California Probate Code § 16061.8, you have 120 days from the date you're served with a Notice of Trust Administration to file a petition contesting a living trust. This deadline is strict—once it passes, the court is generally barred from hearing any new contest. Filing on time is crucial because missing the deadline can permanently prevent you from challenging the trust.

If the trustee provides a copy of the trust along with the notice, the 120-day rule begins on the date of service. However, if the trustee does not include a copy of the trust, the law grants an additional 60 days from the day you receive it.

For example, if you are served with a Notice of Trust Administration on **April 1, 2025**, your deadline to file a petition is **July 30, 2025** (120 days later). However, if the trustee does not provide a copy of the trust when serving the notice, and you do not receive it until **June 10, 2025**, the law grants **an additional 60 days** from the date you receive the trust (Cal. Prob. Code § 16061.8).

In this case, the new deadline would be **August 9, 2025** (60 days from June 10). To visualize how this works, see Figure 3.1, *Filing Deadline Example*.

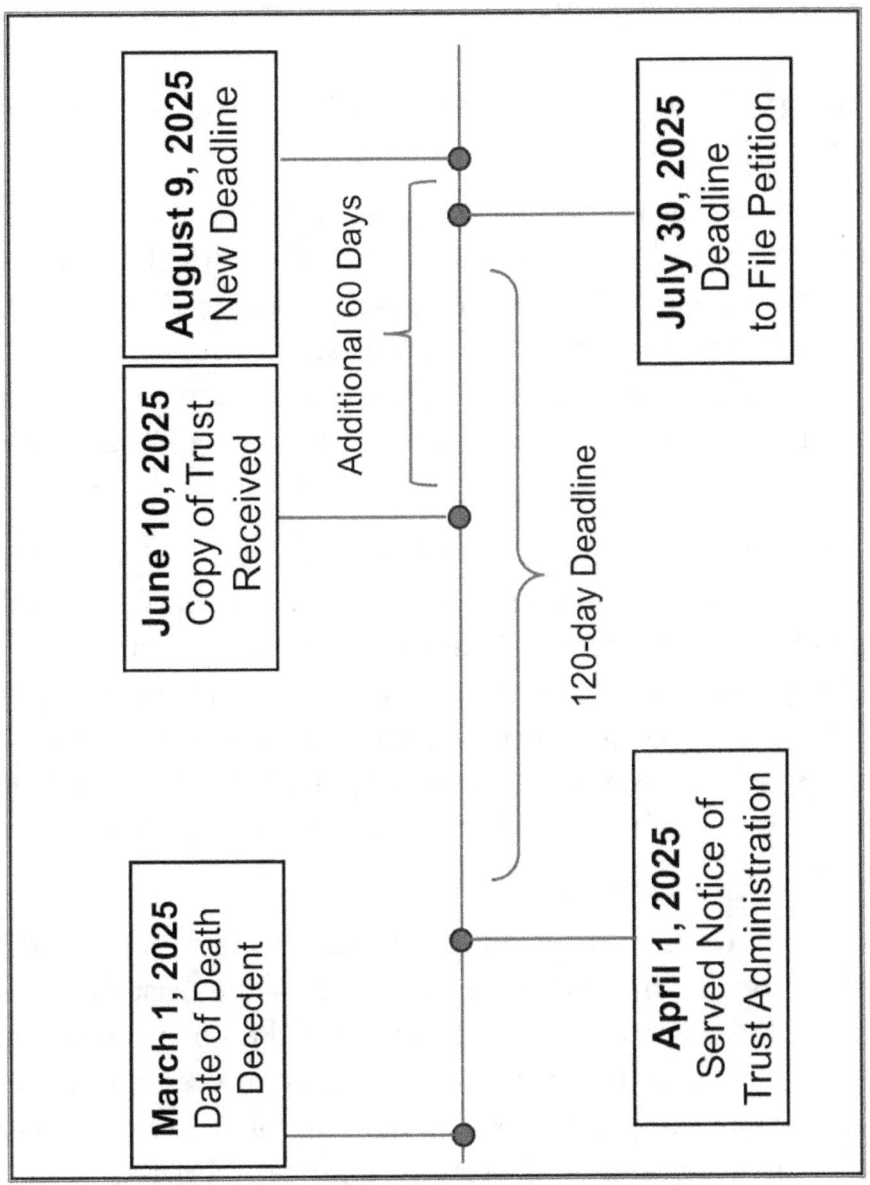

Figure 3.1. Filing Deadline Example
Note. This timeline shows how the 120-day deadline can be extended by 60 days if the trust is received after the notice.

Section 1 – Missed Notices & Starting the Clock

What If You Weren't Served a Notice or a Copy of the Trust?

If you were never served a Notice of Trust Administration, the 120-day rule to contest the trust *never starts*, which means you may still be able to file a petition, even long after the person has passed away. Some trustees skip this step either by mistake or intentionally, especially when trying to keep others in the dark. But without formal service, the court generally won't enforce the 120-day rule.

If you were served with a Notice of Trust Administration but *never received a copy of the trust,* you may still have time to file a petition. Under Probate Code § 16061.8, the 120-day rule does not fully kick in unless the trustee also provides the terms of the trust, which typically means a complete copy. If the trust was never sent, the law gives you *60 days from the date you actually receive it*, even if that's well after the 120-day deadline from the notice.

In this case, you can still file a trust contest and include a declaration or other evidence showing that the trust was never provided to you. Examples include: a signed proof of service that does *not* mention the trust, email records, or even a statement under penalty of perjury explaining that you never received it. The burden may shift to the trustee to prove otherwise.

When Does the Clock Start for Will Objections?

Once a Petition for Probate is filed and the court sets a hearing date, the petitioner (usually the proposed executor) must serve a Notice of Petition to Administer Estate (Form DE-121) to all heirs and beneficiaries. This notice must be delivered *at least 15 days before the hearing.*

The "clock" for filing a will objection (also called a will contest) typically starts once that notice is served. The safest, and most effective, time to object is *before or at the initial probate hearing*, because the court will often admit the will and appoint the executor at that first hearing if no one objects.

However, if you were not properly served (or never received notice), you may still be able to file a will contest after probate is opened, but only for a limited time. Under *California Probate Code § 8004(b),* you have *120 days after the will is admitted to probate* to file a will contest, but only if you didn't have notice before the hearing.

> **Tip:** You can object verbally at the hearing, but you'll usually need to follow up with a formal written petition.

Step 2 – Common Deadlines for Misconduct

Fraud Claims Involving a Trust or Estate

Fraud occurs when someone initially deceives others to gain an unfair advantage, such as forging documents or concealing important information. If you believe someone committed fraud involving a will, trust, or estate administration, you can bring that claim in *probate court* as part of your petition. This might include forging a trust amendment, concealing a will, lying to other heirs, or misleading the court. In California, the general deadline is three years from the date you discovered the fraud, or the date the court determines you reasonably should have discovered it. This is called the discovery rule.

> **Example.** If a sibling secretly filed a fake trust amendment in 2020 and you only discovered it in 2024 while reviewing old paperwork, you may still be able to file a petition alleging fraud in probate court-even if several years have passed.

Breach of Fiduciary Duty by a Trustee or Executor

A **breach of fiduciary duty** occurs when a trustee or executor fails to act in the best interests of the beneficiaries, violating their legal obligations. This may include failing to account for assets, mismanaging property, or engaging in self-dealing.

You can also file a petition in probate court if the trustee or executor violates their legal duties. For example, by failing to account for assets, mismanaging property, or acting in their own interest. These cases are also subject to a discovery rule. If fraud or concealment is involved, the deadline is typically *three years* from when you found out. If the breach involves ordinary negligence or failure to perform duties (like not filing taxes or delaying distributions), you generally have *four years* from discovery.

> **Example.** Say a trustee sold your parent's home in 2021 and never accounted for the money. If you only learned about the sale in 2024 after reviewing a title report, the court may treat 2024 as the start of your timeline to file.

Section 3 – Rejected or Dismissed Petitions

What Happens If Your Petition Is Rejected?

Filing before the deadline is critical, but even timely petitions can be rejected by the court, and the consequences depend on why it was rejected and what type of petition you're filing.

If you filed before the legal deadline but made a *procedural error*, such as missing documents, incorrect formatting, or forgetting to sign, most probate courts will allow you to fix the issue and refile, especially if the case hasn't yet been heard. In this situation, your timely filing preserves your rights, even if the paperwork needs corrections. This applies whether you're contesting a will, challenging a trust, or alleging breach of fiduciary duty by a trustee or executor.

However, if your petition is rejected for a substantive *legal reason*, such as failing to allege valid legal grounds like undue influence, lack of capacity, fraud, or misconduct. The court may dismiss your case entirely. In these situations, the dismissal may be *with prejudice* or *without prejudice*, which determines whether you can file again.

Dismissal Without Prejudice

If the court dismisses your petition **without prejudice**, it means you're being given another chance. "Without prejudice" simply means the court has not made a final judgment (has not pre-judged) on the legal issue. It is dismissing the case for now, but you can try again. As long as you're still within the deadline, you can fix the errors and refile.

> **Example.** You file a petition alleging breach of fiduciary duty but forget to include key financial records or facts. The court dismisses it without prejudice, allowing you to correct and refile-so long as you act before the filing deadline expires.

Dismissal With Prejudice

If the court dismisses your petition **with prejudice**, it means the judge has already ruled that your case has no legal merit, and it cannot be refiled. The court has effectively pre-judged the issue and determined that it cannot move forward again. This often happens when the petition fails to state a recognized legal cause of action, or the court determines the facts you presented, even if true, don't support the relief you're asking for.

> **Example.** You file a petition contesting a will, but your only reason is that the decedent left more money to a sibling, and you feel it's unfair. The court may dismiss the petition *with prejudice,* since unfairness alone isn't legal grounds for a will contest.

Because of this, it is crucial that you present a solid legal case from the beginning. Be sure to carefully review Chapter 9, which covers the legal grounds for a petition. Understanding these legal principles will help you avoid mistakes that could lead to dismissal and permanently losing your case.

Section 4 – Tolling (Pausing) the Clock

Does Filing Pause the Deadline?

Yes. Filing a petition before the deadline pauses the clock. Whether you're challenging a trust under the 120-day rule, contesting a will before probate is granted, or pursuing breach of fiduciary duty within the statute of limitations, a timely petition will preserve your right to be heard, even if your petition needs corrections.

However, filing on time doesn't guarantee success. Your petition still must meet legal requirements. Courts may allow procedural corrections, but if your case lacks proper legal grounds, it may still be dismissed.

Section 5 – How Deadlines Apply in Real Life

How This Works in Practice
To understand how filing deadlines and corrections work, let's look at a few scenarios.

Trust Contest Example
You file a petition 100 days after receiving the Notice of Trust Administration but forget to include a required attachment. The court rejects the petition as incomplete but allows you to refile. Because you filed on time, your right to contest is preserved.

Will Contest Example

You attend the probate hearing and object verbally, then follow up with a written petition. The court finds your initial filing vague but dismisses the case without prejudice, giving you time to refile properly.

Breach of Duty Example

In 2024, you learn that a trustee sold your parent's home in 2021 without disclosure or distribution of funds. You file a petition alleging breach of fiduciary duty. If the court finds your petition lacks evidence of misconduct, it may dismiss the case with or without prejudice depending on how it's presented.

Fraud Example

You allege fraud but fail to support it with dates or facts, and you're filing years after the event with no explanation. The court may dismiss your case with prejudice, finding it untimely and insufficiently pleaded.

Section 6 – Strategy & Case Strength

Avoiding Mistakes and Strengthening Your Case

To improve your chances of filing successfully, it's important to follow best practices. Filing early ensures you have time to fix any issues before the deadline. Waiting until the last minute can leave you without enough time to correct errors.

Additionally, each probate court may have slightly different rules regarding filing, formatting, and service of documents. Checking your local court's website or self-help center can provide valuable guidance.

Before submitting your petition, carefully review all required forms, ensuring that names, dates, and case numbers are accurate. Clearly state your legal grounds, such as undue influence or lack of capacity, and include all necessary attachments.

If you're unsure about procedural requirements, don't hesitate to seek guidance from the probate court's self-help center or website. Many courts offer resources specifically for self-represented litigants.

Finally, if the court flags an issue in your filing, address it immediately. Courts are often lenient with pro per litigants who demonstrate a good-faith effort to comply with the rules.

Conclusion

Meeting the 120-day deadline to contest a trust is non-negotiable in California. Filing on time protects your right to be heard, even if you need to make corrections later. Whether you're contesting a trust, challenging a will, or holding a fiduciary accountable, staying proactive and filing before the deadline is your first critical step. Review your documents carefully, understand your legal grounds, and seek guidance when needed to make sure your case can move forward.

To help solidify these key concepts, Figure 3.2 summarizes the most important takeaways from this chapter on meeting the 120-day deadline (see Figure 3.2, *Key Takeaways – Understanding Deadlines*).

1. You have 120 days from the date you're served with a Notice of Trust Administration to file a contest. If the trust document is served later, you have 60 days from the date of receipt—whichever is later.
2. If you were never properly served, the 120-day deadline may not apply, potentially giving you more time to file even years later.
3. You typically have 120 days from the will's admission to probate to file an objection unless you were properly served before the initial hearing.
4. For fraud, you generally have three years from the date of discovery. For breach of fiduciary duty, the timeline is typically four years—but both may vary depending on the circumstances.
5. If your petition is dismissed "without prejudice," you can correct errors and refile within the original deadline. Dismissal "with prejudice" means the court has determined your case lacks legal merit, preventing you from refiling.
6. Submitting your petition before the deadline preserves your right to pursue the case, even if corrections are needed later.
7. File as early as possible. Carefully review your paperwork and respond promptly to any issues flagged by the court.

Figure 3.2. Key Takeaways – Understanding Deadlines
Summarizes key deadlines and procedural strategies to preserve your right to contest trusts, wills, and fiduciary actions in California probate.

CHAPTER 4

Who Has Standing?

Introduction

Before you can contest a trust or will in probate court, you must first establish that you have legal standing. Simply put, **standing** means you have the right to challenge the document because you are directly affected by its terms. Probate courts don't allow just anyone to file a dispute; only those with a legitimate, legally recognized interest can bring a case. Failing to establish standing can result in your case being dismissed before it even begins.

In this chapter, we'll explore who qualifies as an "interested person" under California law, how to prove your standing if it's disputed, and what to do if the opposing party challenges your right to contest. Understanding the rules of standing will help you build a strong foundation for your case and ensure your voice is heard.

Understanding Your Right to Contest a Trust or Will

Before filing a petition to contest a trust or will, you must determine whether you have **legal standing**, that is, the right to bring a lawsuit or challenge in court. Probate courts do not allow just anyone to contest an estate plan; only individuals with a direct, personal, and legally recognized interest can file. If you do not meet the legal definition of an "interested party," the court may dismiss your case before it even begins.

Recent cases like *Barefoot v. Jennings (2020)* and *Estate of Lind (1989)* have clarified that even disinherited individuals may have standing if they can demonstrate a legitimate connection to the estate or allege undue influence or lack of capacity.

Who Can Contest a Trust or Will?

Standing is typically granted to individuals who are directly affected by the trust or will. This includes named beneficiaries in either the current or a prior version of the estate plan, as well as heirs-at-law, such as spouses, children, parents, or siblings, who would inherit if the document were invalidated. Even someone who was removed or had their inheritance reduced in a later version may have grounds to contest, particularly if the changes resulted from undue influence, lack of capacity, or fraud. Even current beneficiaries may contest a trust or will if they believe it was improperly executed or altered under suspicious circumstances.

Heirs-at-law, such as spouses, children, parents, or siblings, also have standing if they would inherit under **intestacy laws** in the absence of a valid will or trust. If a trust or will unfairly disinherited them, they may be able to argue that it was the result of coercion or undue influence. Additionally, creditors of the estate may have standing if they can show that assets were improperly transferred to avoid paying debts. In some cases, trustees or fiduciaries responsible for managing a related trust or estate may also have standing to challenge an estate plan, particularly if it conflicts with their legal duties.

The California Supreme Court in *Barefoot v. Jennings (2020)* held that at the early pleading stage, courts must take allegations of undue influence or lack of capacity as true when evaluating standing. Similarly, *Estate of Lind (1989)* allows standing for disinherited heirs if they were named in a previous version of the will or trust.

The Challenge of Disinherited Beneficiaries

One of the most common standing challenges occurs when a person has been disinherited. Many assume that if they were removed from a trust or will, they have no right to contest it, but that is not always true. Courts recognize that some changes to an estate plan happen under suspicious circumstances, such as undue influence, lack of capacity, or fraud. If a person was included in a previous version of the trust or will but later removed, they may have standing to challenge the changes. However, this issue often becomes the first legal battle in a probate case.

The California Supreme Court in *Barefoot v. Jennings (2020)* clarified that being disinherited does not necessarily eliminate standing if the petitioner can show they were improperly removed from the estate plan. Additionally, *Estate of Simmonds (1972)* establishes that heirs at law may still contest a will if they would inherit under intestacy in the absence of the contested document.

Under California law, certain individuals are legally defined as "interested persons" who may contest a trust or will under *Probate Code § 48* (see Figure 4.1, *Who Qualifies as an Interested Person*).

- **Heirs-at-law** – Individuals who would inherit under intestacy laws if there were no valid will or trust. This includes biological and adopted children, spouses, parents, and siblings of the decedent. Even a disinherited heirs can still qualify as interested persons.
- **Beneficiaries** – Anyone named in the current version of a trust or will. This includes both specific beneficiaries (who receive a set amount) and residual beneficiaries (who receive what remains after distributions).
- **Individuals named in prior versions of a trust or will** – Even if someone was removed from the most recent version of a trust, they may still be considered an interested person. This is especially relevant when changes to an estate plan appear to have been made under undue influence, duress, or lack of capacity.
- **Fiduciaries and executors** – Trustee or executors named in a prior estate plans who were later removed may be considered an interested person.
- **Creditors** – Individuals or businesses with a legal claim against the estate, such as unpaid debts.

Figure 4.1. Who Qualifies as an "Interested Person" Under California Probate Code § 48.
This figure summarizes the main categories of people who may have standing in probate court under § 48, including heirs, beneficiaries (current or former), fiduciaries, and creditors.

Our Story: Fighting for Standing

After filing our petition, we were served with a motion to dismiss from the opposing attorney, citing *Barefoot v. Jennings*. Their argument was that, because we were no longer named beneficiaries, we had no legal right to challenge the trust. If granted, this motion would have ended our case before we even had a chance to present evidence.

We knew we had to fight back. In our Objection to the Motion to Dismiss, we pointed out that Barefoot specifically states that when evaluating standing, the court must take allegations of undue influence or lack of capacity as true. We argued that we had a direct interest in the estate as biological children of the decedent, which established our standing. To support this, we cited Probate Code § 48, which defines an "interested person" to include heirs and beneficiaries, even those named in prior versions of a trust.

We also argued that the Respondent had already acknowledged us as heirs when he served us with a Notification by Trustee, explicitly stating that we were disinherited, and he was the sole beneficiary. This notice was issued under Probate Code § 16061.7, the very same statute the Respondent relied on in his argument. If the trustee had no obligation to notify us, then why did he serve us? His own actions contradicted his claim that we lacked standing.

Most importantly, we pointed to the California Supreme Court ruling in Barefoot v. Jennings, which made clear that, at this stage, that lower courts must take claims of lack of capacity and undue influence as true when determining standing. Since our

> petition raised both claims, the court could not dismiss our case without first considering these allegations.
>
> At our hearing, the judge ruled in our favor, denying the motion to dismiss and allowing our case to move forward. It was our first major victory. Although there were still many legal hurdles ahead, overcoming this motion meant that we had the right to be heard in court.

How to Fight for Standing if It's Disputed

When the opposing party challenges standing, it is crucial to demonstrate why you have a valid claim. Courts will consider evidence such as previous versions of the trust or will, medical history, and the circumstances surrounding the changes. If you have been disinherited, proving that the changes were made under undue influence or while the decedent lacked capacity can strengthen your argument. Even if you are not a named beneficiary in the most recent version, you may be able to establish standing by showing a clear connection to the estate and providing evidence that the changes should be questioned.

Standing is just the first hurdle in contesting a trust or will. The next section will explore the legal grounds for a challenge, including undue influence, lack of capacity, and fraud.

> **Note for Will-Based Cases.** If you're contesting a will rather than a trust, the notification process is different. In California, heirs and beneficiaries of a will are notified using a *Notice of Petition to Administer Estate* (Form DE-121), as required under *Probate Code § 8110*. This must be served before the initial court hearing and serves a similar role to the trustee notification in trust-based cases.

Conclusion

Being disinherited doesn't necessarily mean you lack standing. Courts consider more than just the latest version of a trust or will. They look at prior versions, the mental state of the decedent, and whether suspicious circumstances like undue influence or fraud were involved. If someone tries to shut your case down early with a motion to dismiss, don't panic. That's a common legal tactic, and you have the right to respond with strong legal arguments and evidence. California Probate Code § 48 is your starting point, and the Supreme Court's decision in *Barefoot v. Jennings* adds powerful support. If you were served with a Notification of Trust under Probate Code § 16061.7, the trustee has already recognized you as an heir. The road ahead may still be long, but winning the fight for standing is your first and most important step forward.

The following key takeaways in Figure 4.2 summarize the most important concepts from this chapter, including who has standing in probate cases, how to respond to standing challenges, and the relevant legal standards to keep in mind (see Figure 4.2, - *Who Has Standing?*).

1. Being disinherited doesn't necessarily prevent someone from contesting a will or trust. Courts may still consider a challenge if the person was named in a prior version or would inherit under intestate succession.
2. Standing in trust and will contests is often litigated under California's Barefoot v. Jennings and Probate Code § 17200. The California Supreme Court held that, at the pleading stage, courts must assume allegations of undue influence or lack of capacity as true when evaluating standing.
3. Respondents often file motions to dismiss in an effort to end a case early. A petitioner may need to counter by presenting earlier versions of the estate plan versions or evidence supporting undue influence or incapacity.
4. Probate Code § 48 defines "interested persons." This includes heirs, current or former beneficiaries, fiduciaries, and creditors.
5. For trusts, heirs and beneficiaries are typically notified under Probate Code § 16061.7. This notice may support their role as interested persons.
6. For wills, notice is usually provided through a Notice of Petition to Administer Estate (Form DE-121). This follows Probate Code § 8110 requirements.

Figure 4.2. Key Takeaways – Who Has Standing?
Summarizes legal standing in California probate, including key Probate Code sections and Barefoot v. Jennings. Covers both will and trust contests, plus common challenges like motions to dismiss. For educational purposes only—not legal advice.

CHAPTER 5

Do You Have a Strong Case?

Introduction

Filing a petition to contest a trust or will is a significant legal step, and not every grievance meets the legal standard for a challenge. To build a strong case, you must understand the specific legal grounds, such as undue influence, lack of capacity, fraud, improper execution, financial elder abuse, or breach of fiduciary duty, and gather substantial evidence to support your claim. This chapter breaks down these legal concepts and provides guidance on collecting the right evidence to substantiate your case.

This chapter is designed to help you assess whether your situation meets these legal criteria. While not every case will meet the necessary standard, understanding the evidence required for each claim can help you make an informed decision before filing.

> **Disclaimer.** This chapter is for educational purposes only. It does not provide legal advice and is not a substitute for consulting an attorney. Every probate case is unique, and the examples or explanations here may not apply to your specific situation. If you are unsure whether you have a valid legal claim, consider seeking professional legal guidance.

What Are the Legal Grounds for Contesting a Trust or Will?

A person cannot challenge a trust or will simply because they believe the decedent made a poor decision or treated beneficiaries unfairly. Instead, probate courts require a legally recognized basis to consider overturning an estate plan. These legal grounds are rooted in the idea that the decedent either did not have the capacity to make decisions, was improperly influenced or deceived, or that legal procedures were not properly followed.

The most common legal grounds for contesting a trust or will include undue influence, lack of capacity, fraud, improper execution, financial elder abuse, and breach of fiduciary duty (see Table 5.1, *Legal Grounds for Contesting a Trust or Will*). Each of these claims requires specific types of evidence and is based on distinct legal definitions.

Table 5.1. Common Legal Grounds for Contesting a Trust or Will

Legal Ground	What it Means
Undue Influence	The decedent was manipulated, coerced, or deceived into making estate changes.
Lack of Capacity	The decedent didn't understand what they were signing at the time it was signed.
Fraud	The decedent was tricked into signing a trust or will through forgery or deception.
Improper Execution	The estate plan did not meet legal requirements, e.g., missing signatures or witnesses.
Financial elder abuse	An individual exploited the decedent for financial gain.
Breach of fiduciary duty	A fiduciary failed to act in the best interests of the decedent or beneficiaries—by mismanaging assets, withholding information, pr self-dealing.

Note. This table outlines the legal grounds for contesting a trust or will. Each claim must be supported by evidence and involves specific legal criteria that the court will evaluate.

These claims are not interchangeable, but they often overlap in complex cases. For example, someone who exerts undue influence may also commit financial elder abuse or fraud. Because the burden of proof is on the petitioner, understanding these legal grounds and the kinds of evidence courts typically consider is essential before moving forward.

Collect Evidence: Evidence Checklist

Before asserting your legal claims, review the Evidence Checklist to identify the types of proof that can support your case. Think of it as your fact-finding companion—it helps you gather documents, records, and observations that align with each legal ground and increase your petition's credibility.

> **Build Your Evidence.** Use the **Evidence Checklist** to start gathering what you'll need. Download it at https://properprobate.guide/california-filing or scan  the QR code. It walks you through collecting the proof you'll need to strengthen your case before you file in court.

Undue Influence

Undue influence occurs when a person in a position of power manipulates, coerces, or deceives the decedent, leading to an estate plan that does not reflect the decedent's true wishes. Unlike simple persuasion, undue influence overpowers the decedent's free will, causing them to make decisions they would not have otherwise made. This often happens when the decedent is vulnerable due to age, illness, dependency, or isolation and is pressured by someone who stands to benefit from changes to their estate plan.

To determine whether undue influence was present, courts evaluate four legal criteria: (1) the decedent's vulnerability, (2) the influencer's actions, (3) the influencer's position of apparent authority, and (4) the fairness of the estate plan's outcome (*Cal. Welf. & Inst. Code § 15610.70*; *Estate of Sarabia, 221 Cal. App. 3d 599, 1990*; *Smith, 2023*). Some pieces of evidence may apply to multiple categories. For example, if a trustee sells estate property in secrecy without informing other beneficiaries, this could be categorized as both actions and tactics of the influencer (because they concealed information and controlled decision-making) and apparent authority (because they exercised unilateral control over the estate).

To establish undue influence in probate court, petitioners must show that four distinct legal criteria are present. These elements are not standalone. They work together to help the court determine whether the decedent's true wishes were overridden. Figure 5.1 illustrates how these four elements contribute to a finding of undue influence (see Figure 5.1, *The Four Elements of Undue Influence*).

The first element is **vulnerability of the victim**, meaning the individual was susceptible to influence due to cognitive decline, illness, dependency, advanced age, or social isolation.

Next, courts look at the **apparent authority of the influencer** refers to the influencer's position of trust or power, such as being a caregiver, close family member, legal advisor, or someone the decedent relied on.

The third criterion is the **actions and tactics of the influencer**, including whether the person used deception, excessive persuasion, manipulation, or intimidation to gain control over the decedent's decisions.

Finally, the court considers the **inequity of the result**, including whether the resulting trust or will changes seem unnatural, suspicious, or unjustified, such as suddenly disinheriting long-standing beneficiaries in favor of a single person.

Each of these four elements contributes to a compelling case. While not every situation meets all four, the presence of multiple factors strengthens the argument that undue influence occurred. Use these guidelines to assess whether your situation aligns with the legal standards for undue influence.

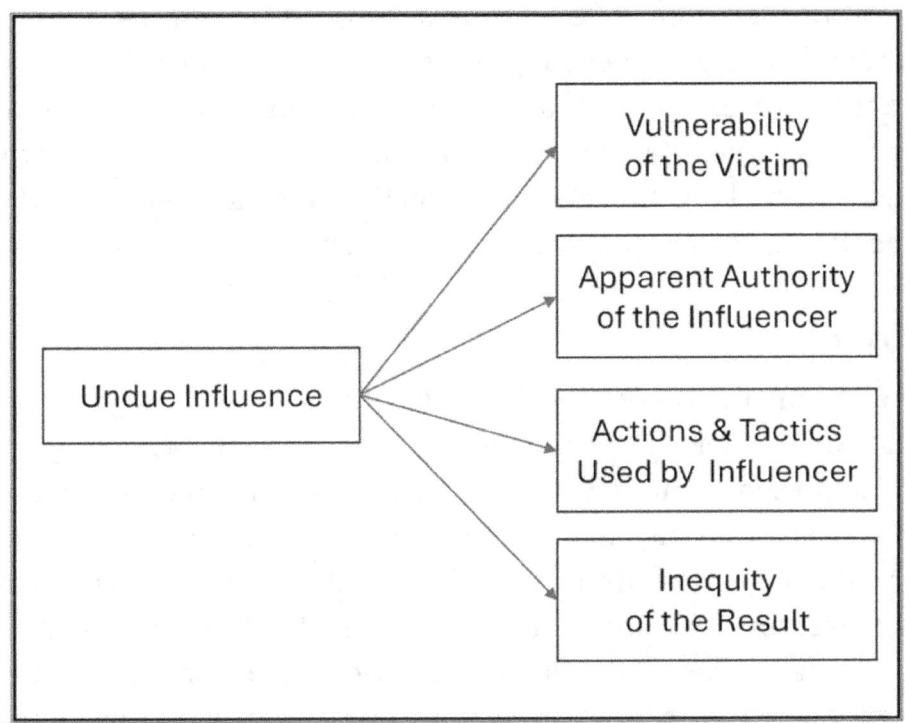

Figure 5.1. The Four Elements of Undue Influence
Legal criteria that support a finding of undue influence. Courts evaluate whether the decedent was vulnerable, whether the influencer used manipulative tactics, whether the influencer had a position of authority, and whether the result was unfair. All four elements are considered together to determine whether undue influence took place.

Lack of Capacity

A **lack of capacity** claim argues that the decedent was mentally incapable of understanding the nature of their estate plan at the time of signing. A valid trust or will requires that the decedent *understood* what they were signing, *recognized* their heirs and beneficiaries, and *made decisions freely*, without external control.

If the decedent suffered from dementia, Alzheimer's disease, or another cognitive impairment, they may have lacked the legal capacity to execute estate documents. Courts look at medical records, witness testimony, and evidence of confusion or erratic decision-making to determine whether the decedent had the mental capacity required to make estate planning decisions.

Fraud

Fraud involves deception that causes the decedent to sign a trust or will under false pretenses. This can include forgery, misrepresentation, or tricking the decedent into signing a document they did not understand. For example, if a person fraudulently presents a trust document to the decedent, and representing it is a different legal document, this could invalidate the estate plan. Because direct evidence of fraud is rare, petitioners must rely on circumstantial evidence, including handwriting analysis, witness testimony, and inconsistencies in the decedent's prior statements about their intentions.

Improper Execution

Improper execution occurs when a trust or will fails to meet the legal formalities required by state law. Common errors include missing signatures, lack of proper witnesses, or failure to notarize the document where required. If an estate plan was created under suspicious circumstances, such as without legal counsel or with significant involvement from the primary beneficiary, courts may scrutinize whether it was properly executed.

Financial Elder Abuse

Financial elder abuse is a separate but related claim, often arising when someone exploits an elderly person for financial gain. This could involve pressuring the decedent to make financial gifts, changing account access, or exerting control over assets before death. If financial abuse resulted in changes to a trust or will, petitioners may argue that the estate plan was a product of coercion and should be invalidated.

Breach of Fiduciary Duty

A **breach of fiduciary duty** is when a fiduciary, such as a trustee, executor, or power of attorney, is legally obligated to act in the best interests of the decedent and all beneficiaries. Breach of fiduciary duty occurs when that person acts in their own interest instead, mismanages estate assets, withholds information, or violates legal responsibilities. Examples include failing to provide a proper accounting, selling property without disclosure, commingling funds, or making distributions that favor one beneficiary over others. This is a common claim in probate when a trustee has sole control of the estate and others are left in the dark.

Gathering Evidence to Support Your Claim

Filing a petition is only the beginning. To succeed in probate court, you must be prepared to support your legal claims with clear, credible evidence. Courts require more than suspicion or family conflict. They rely on documents, testimony, and records that show something improper occurred. The type of evidence needed depends on the nature of your claim. For example, a case based on lack of capacity will require different documentation than a case involving breach of fiduciary duty. **Figure 5.2** provides an overview of the kinds of evidence commonly used to support different legal grounds when contesting a trust or will (see Figure 5.1, *Common Types of Evidence to Support Claim*).

<u>Undue Influence</u>
- ☐ Medical records
- ☐ Witness testimony
- ☐ Emails/Texts from the decedent
- ☐ Sudden changes in estate plans
- ☐ Isolation

<u>Lack of Capacity</u>
- ☐ Doctor evaluations
- ☐ Hospital records
- ☐ Statements from family
- ☐ Legal documents

<u>Fraud</u>
- ☐ Handwriting analysis
- ☐ Prior estate plans
- ☐ Deceptive communications

<u>Improper Execution</u>
- ☐ Missing signatures
- ☐ Invalid Notary records
- ☐ Attorney statements

<u>Financial Elder Abuse</u>
- ☐ Bank records
- ☐ Sudden financial changes
- ☐ Self-dealing

<u>Breach of Fiduciary Duty</u>
- ☐ Bank statements
- ☐ IRS documents
- ☐ Emails or text
- ☐ Property transfer records
- ☐ Formal trust accountings

Figure 5.2. Types of Evidence to Support Claim
Examples of documentation that may support a trust or will contest. The relevance depends on your legal claim (e.g., undue influence, fraud, or breach of duty). Use this list as a starting point when organizing your evidence before filing.

How to Self-Evaluate

Before moving forward with a legal challenge, take time to review your evidence and assess its strength. Use the checklist provided (see Figure 5.3, *Evaluating the Strength of Your Case*) as a tool to gather your thoughts and organize your documentation. While this is not a guarantee of success, it can help determine whether your case has the foundation necessary to move forward.

The Importance of Evidence: Direct vs. Circumstantial

There is a presumption of validity for the most recent trust or will, meaning it is considered legally binding unless proven otherwise. This places the burden on the petitioner to present convincing evidence of undue influence, fraud, or another legal defect. However, direct evidence, such as a clear statement from the decedent admitting they were coerced or lacked capacity, is exceedingly rare.

Many individuals under undue influence do not realize they are being manipulated. Coercion often happens in private, away from witnesses. Those experiencing cognitive decline may not recognize their own limitations, and fear, dependency, or isolation can keep them from speaking out. For these reasons, proving undue influence or fraud through direct testimony alone is extremely difficult.

Instead, these cases often rely on **circumstantial evidence** to demonstrate improper conduct. Common indicators include medical records documenting dementia or cognitive impairment, sudden or unexplained changes to estate planning documents, financial transactions that disproportionately benefit one person, and testimony from friends, caregivers, or family members noting signs of manipulation or isolation.

A strong case does not hinge on a single document or moment. Rather, it is built from a combination of factors that, when viewed together, paint a compelling picture of undue influence or fraud. The more inconsistencies, suspicious actions, or unexplained changes a petitioner can present, the stronger their argument becomes.

Conclusion

A well-written petition is only as strong as the evidence that supports it. Courts don't act on emotion. They act on facts. While probate cases are deeply personal, the court's job is to apply the law objectively, not repair family wounds. That's why it's essential to critically evaluate your evidence and legal grounds before deciding to file a petition. Taking this first step helps ensure that your case has a solid foundation, increasing the likelihood of being heard in court.

Contesting a trust or will is not about checking boxes, but sometimes, reviewing what you *do* have can bring clarity. The checklist in Figure 5.3 is not a test or a guarantee of success. Instead, it offers a starting point for gathering your thoughts and evidence. It may also help you recognize where you need to dig deeper, ask more questions, or seek advice.

> - ❏ I have medical records showing cognitive impairment or a dementia diagnosis.
> - ❏ I have emails, texts, or voicemails that suggest manipulation, control, or secrecy.
> - ❏ I can identify sudden or unexplained changes to the estate plan.
> - ❏ I have financial records showing unusual transfers or account changes.
> - ❏ The trustee, executor, or power of attorney has not provided a full accounting.
> - ❏ Property was sold or transferred without notice to other beneficiaries.
> - ❏ I have testimony or written statements from witnesses who observed changes in behavior or isolation.
> - ❏ The trust or will was signed under questionable conditions (e.g., no attorney, rushed signing, unusual witnesses).
> - ❏ I have evidence the influencer was in a position of power or control over the decedent.

Figure 5.3. Evaluating the Strength of Your Case
This checklist helps you identify common red flags and types of evidence courts may consider in probate disputes, including claims of undue influence, lack of capacity, or breach of fiduciary duty. Use it as a personal tool to organize documentation and assess your readiness to move forward.

Figure 5.4 highlights the key takeaways from Chapter 5, summarizing the essential points to consider when evaluating whether you have a strong case to contest a trust or will (see Figure 5.4, *Key Takeaways – Building a Strong Case*).

1. Not all unfair outcomes justify a legal challenge. Valid grounds include undue influence, lack of capacity, fraud, improper execution, financial elder abuse, or breach of fiduciary duty.
2. Undue influence requires four elements: the decedent's vulnerability, the influencer's authority, their actions, and the inequity of the result.
3. Lack of capacity means the decedent couldn't understand the nature or consequences of the document signed. This may result from cognitive decline or illness.
4. Fraud and improper execution focus on deception and formal errors. Fraud involves misleading the decedent; improper execution means failing to meet legal requirements.
5. Financial elder abuse involves exploiting the decedent for financial gain. It often overlaps with undue influence.
6. Breach of fiduciary duty occurs when a trustee or executor acts in their own interest. This includes mismanaging assets or withholding information.
7. Evidence is crucial. Combine direct evidence (such as medical records or witness declarations) and circumstantial evidence (such as banking activity or caregiver control) to strengthen your case.

Figure 5.4. Key Takeaways – Building a Strong Case
Summarizes key elements to consider before contesting a trust or will—legal grounds, evidence, and strategy tips. For general guidance only; not legal advice.

CHAPTER 6

When You Might Be Doing This Alone

Introduction

Navigating a probate dispute without legal representation can feel overwhelming, but it's a reality many people face. Hiring an attorney might seem like the ideal solution, but the cost can be prohibitive—especially for smaller estates or contested matters. Understanding why attorneys often decline cases and what it means for your path forward is essential. This chapter explores the financial challenges of hiring probate counsel, why self-representation might be your only option, and practical steps to move forward when you're on your own.

Why Legal Representations Isn't Always an Option

Why Lawyers Won't Take Small Estate Cases

Many people assume that hiring a lawyer will make probate easier, but for small or moderately sized estates, it can be surprisingly hard to find one willing to take the case. This isn't necessarily because the case lacks merit; more often, it's because of how attorneys are paid.

In *uncontested matters*, probate attorneys often charge what's known as a *statutory fee*, based on the gross value of the estate rather than the net value after debts are subtracted. These fees are outlined in California Probate Code § 10810 (2025) and follow a specific tiered structure: 4% of the first $100,000, 3% of the next $100,000, and 2% of the next $800,000. So, for example, a $500,000 estate would result in about $13,000 in attorney's fees. If the estate is worth $1 million, that number jumps to roughly $23,000.

Probate attorneys often charge a statutory fee based on the gross value of the estate (see Table 6.1, *Statutory Fees (California)*).

Table 6.1. Statutory Fees (California)

Estate Value	Fee %	Total
First $100,000	4%	$4,000
Next $100,000 ($100k-$200k)	3%	$3,000
Next $800,000 ($200k-$1M)	2%	$16,000
Total for $1,000,000 estate		$23,000

Note. Statutory fees for standard probate administration are calculated based on the gross value of the estate and not the net value after debts. These fees, established under California Probate Code §10810 (2025), do not include court filing fees, executor fees, or litigation costs.

Hourly Fees for Contested Matters

If the case is *contested*, the statutory fee doesn't apply. Instead, attorneys charge by the hour, often ranging from $300 to $850 per hour depending on location and experience. In places like Los Angeles or San Francisco, it's not unusual for hourly rates to exceed $500. Initial retainers for contested matters can run between $10,000 and $50,000 or more. If the case goes to trial, the total costs can easily exceed $100,000.

These numbers are daunting for most families, particularly those facing complex or emotionally charged probate disputes. As shown in *Table 6.2, Estimated Probate Litigation Costs*

(California), typical costs for probate litigation can be substantial.

Table 6.2. Estimated Probate Litigation Costs (California)

Cost Category	Estimated Range	Notes
Hourly Attorney Fees	$300-$800/hr.	Lower in rural areas; higher in cities (e.g., LA, SF)
Initial Retainer	$10,000-$50,000+	Paid upfront. Higher for complex cases
Preparations & Discovery	$15,000-$30,000+	Includes subpoenas, depositions, expert review
Motions & Hearings	$10,000-$25,000	Depends on filings and court appearances
Trial (if contested)	$50,000-$100,000+	Trial prep, expert costs, multiple days in court
Total Cost	$75,000-$200,000+	Based on length, complexity, and outcome

Note. Estimates apply to contested probate matters—like trust/will challenges, elder abuse, or fiduciary disputes. Attorneys charge hourly, not statutory, and total costs can rise sharply if the case involves trial or multiple parties.

What Is a Contingency Fee?

In rare cases, an attorney might agree to take your case on something called a *contingency basis*. This means you don't pay them upfront. Instead, they take a percentage (often around 40%) of whatever money you recover at the end of the case. For example, if you win or settle for $500,000, the attorney will keep $200,000, and you'd receive the remaining $300,000.

However, that's not the whole story. Contingency does not always include case costs. Most attorneys will track the costs of filing fees, court reporters, expert witnesses, travel, copying, subpoenas, and other litigation expenses as the case goes on. These expenses, sometimes called "reimbursable costs," are often deducted from your share of the settlement or award. In some cases, these are deducted before the attorney takes their percentage, in others, after. Either way, the final amount you receive could be much lower than the original settlement figure.

Is Contingency Worth It?

For many people, giving up 40% (or more) can feel like too much. But for others, that trade-off is worth it. If the attorney is handling the deadlines, preparing the filings, making the arguments, and showing up in court, and you walk away with money you didn't have before, then the peace of mind may feel like a fair exchange.

Contingency arrangements aren't offered to everyone. Most attorneys only take these types of cases when they involve clear financial wrongdoing (like elder abuse or fraud), strong evidence, and a high likelihood of recovery. They rarely take contingency cases based solely on lack of capacity or undue influence, unless the facts are unusually strong and the estate is large.

If you find an attorney who is willing to take your case on contingency, it's a good sign—your case likely has merit. And in that situation, you'll have a real decision to make: Do you let them take the lead in exchange for a significant cut? Or do you try to represent yourself and keep more of the outcome (see Table 6.3, *Contingency Representation*)?

Table 6.3. Contingency Representation

Feature	What is Means
Upfront Cost	$0. The attorney covers the costs until recovery.
Attorney's Fee	Typically 40% of your recovery (sometimes higher).
Case Cost	Filing fees, expert witnesses, subpoenas, etc. — usually reimbursed from your share.
Total Recovery Example	$500,000 settlement → approx. $270,000 after fees and costs.
Most Common in Cases of	Financial elder abuse, fraud, or trustee misconduct with clear documentation.
Rare for Cases Involving	Lack of capacity or undue influence without strong evidence.
If Offered	Indicates your case likely has strong legal merit.
If Not Offered	Doesn't mean your case lacks merit, just that it may be harder to prove.

Note. This table outlines key features of contingency representation, including typical inclusions, cost expectations, and the types of cases where attorneys are more or less likely to take on financial risk.

When Attorneys Walk Away from Valid Cases

Sometimes, even when you believe something clearly went wrong, like a loved one signing documents they didn't fully understand or being manipulated into changing a will, attorneys may still turn down the case. That doesn't necessarily mean your concerns aren't valid. It often comes down to proof.

In probate court, *capacity* and *undue influence* are legal standards that require more than gut feelings or family history. What matters is what can be shown through evidence, such as medical records, witness statements, documented patterns of control, or inconsistencies in the estate plan. Without that kind of documentation, even compelling stories can be seen as too risky to litigate.

> **"Just because no one else will fight for you doesn't mean you aren't worth the fight."**
> - Reflection from a self-represented petitioner

Attorneys may also decline cases that involve multiple beneficiaries, family conflict, or emotionally charged disputes that lack clear legal violations. If the case seems uncertain, difficult to prove, or overly dependent on subjective interpretation, many lawyers will simply walk away—not because they don't care, but because they know how high the burden of proof can be.

Our Experience

In our case, we estimated our mother's estate to be worth around $1.5 million. We met with two attorneys from the same law firm, and both declined to take our case. They explained that while our concerns were valid, the case would likely be expensive and difficult to prove. And in the end, it might not be worth pursuing financially.

Then we received the bill for the consultation (over $3,000 for them to tell us no). They charged $350 per hour, and they billed us not just for the meeting itself, but also for the time it took them to review the documents we had sent in advance to get up to speed. At that point, we didn't yet have our mother's medical records or any financial documentation. All we had were some emails, a few text messages, and what we had witnessed firsthand. But we had no hard proof.

Even if they had agreed to represent us, we realized we couldn't afford them. We didn't qualify for free legal aid, but we also couldn't pay tens of thousands of dollars in retainers and litigation fees. The consultation fee alone felt like a gut punch.

Like many others, we found ourselves stuck in a no-man's land—not poor enough to get help, not rich enough to pay for it. And so, we were forced to represent ourselves.

That's why this guide exists: to offer support to people like us—those who believe something wrong may have happened, but who have to go it alone.

What to Do If You're On Your Own

If no attorney is willing to take your case, that doesn't mean it lacks merit. It may simply mean the evidence is harder to prove, or the recovery isn't large enough to justify the risk from their perspective. You may find yourself where many of us do—in the middle: not eligible for free legal help, but unable to pay for private counsel.

Before deciding to represent yourself, consult with a qualified probate attorney who specializes in litigation. Even if an attorney ultimately declines to take your case, the consultation can give you valuable insights into your case's strengths, weaknesses, and potential strategies. Going into the process with professional guidance will help you make an informed decision and prepare for the challenges ahead.

If that's the case, know this: you still have options. Self-representation isn't easy, but it is possible. And that's exactly what this guide is here to support you through.

Ultimately, if a lawyer refuses to take your case, it doesn't necessarily mean it has no merit. It might just mean that the costs, risks, and burden of proof outweigh what's financially or strategically viable in their view.

And for many people, that's when self-representation becomes the only path forward.

The Reality of Going It Alone

If you find yourself pursuing this case without an attorney, it's important to be realistic about the commitment involved. Taking on a probate case as a **pro per** litigant means more than just writing and filing paperwork. It means hours of research, drafting, and organizing.

In my case, I spent over *400 hours* on this case, averaging about 12 hours per month for three years.

Had I hired an attorney to do this work, I would have been billed at around $350 per hour (a lower-end rate for probate litigation). That would have amounted to approximately $140,000—just in legal fees. Of course, not all of that time was spent drafting documents; much of it involved learning the legal concepts and procedures I needed to move the case forward. Still, the time investment was significant.

And honestly, I didn't have a guide like this when I started. Much of my time was spent figuring things out on my own, such as researching statutes, deciphering court rules, making mistakes, and understanding how to draft a legally sound petition. My goal with this guide is to save you that learning curve by providing clear, step-by-step instructions from the start.

Being realistic about the time and effort involved is essential before deciding to proceed without a lawyer. While the cost savings can be substantial, the workload requires commitment, persistence, and the willingness to learn as you go.

Your Path May Be Different—But It's Still Yours

Whether you're unable to find an attorney or simply decide that self-representation is the right path for you, know that you're not alone in facing this dilemma. Many people find themselves priced out of legal help, not because their case lacks merit, but because the system wasn't designed for affordability or nuance.

If an attorney won't take your case, it may just mean the risks are too high or the outcome too uncertain from their perspective. But their "no" isn't the end of the road. With the right knowledge and preparation, you still have a way forward.

This chapter wasn't meant to discourage you. It was meant to equip you. Whether you're working with an attorney, seeking one out, or deciding to stand alone, you deserve clarity, confidence, and choices.

And that's exactly what the rest of this guide is here to offer.

Conclusion

Going it alone in probate court is a daunting prospect, but it doesn't mean your case lacks merit or that you're destined to fail. Often, the choice to represent yourself comes down to practical realities like cost, risk, or lack of available legal support. By understanding the challenges and preparing thoroughly, you can increase your chances of success, even without a lawyer by your side. This chapter aimed to give you clarity on why attorneys may decline your case and how to proceed if self-representation becomes necessary. Stay focused, stay organized, and know that it is possible to move forward on your own terms.

Navigating probate without legal representation can feel overwhelming, but understanding the challenges and options available will help you make more informed decisions (see Figure 6.1, *Key Takeaways – Going It Alone*). Figure 6.1 highlights the key takeaways from this chapter:

1. Finding an attorney for a contested probate case can be difficult, especially if the estate is modest or evidence is limited.
2. For contested cases, attorneys often charge hourly rates for contested cases, ranging from $300 to $850 per hour, with retainers often starting at $10,000 to $50,000—making representation unaffordable for many.
3. Contingency representation (around 40% of recovery) is rare and usually requires a high-value estate and strong evidence.
4. If an attorney declines your case, it doesn't necessarily mean it lacks merit. It may simply reflect the high effort or low return involved, or difficulty proving your claims in court.
5. Representing yourself requires significant time and effort. Be prepared to learn complex legal concepts and manage the case independently.
6. Consult with a qualified probate attorney before proceeding on your own. Understanding your options will help you make an informed decision.

Figure 6.1. Key Takeaways – Going It Alone
Key considerations when going it alone in probate—why hiring a lawyer can be difficult, the cost involved, and what it means to self-represent. Understanding your options helps you make informed choices about whether to proceed with or without legal counsel.

PART III

Filing a Petition

Once you've confirmed your eligibility and gathered the necessary information, the next step is drafting and filing your petition. Before crafting your legal arguments, you must ensure you meet the court's procedural requirements. This section walks you through the petition process, including procedural filing requirements, legal content expectations, and how to ensure your submission is properly formatted and accepted by the court.

CHAPTER 7

Overview of the Filing Process

Introduction

Filing a petition in probate court is a significant step in challenging a trust, will, or fiduciary conduct. While the process may seem daunting, understanding the key steps involved will help you feel more prepared and confident. This chapter provides a clear overview of the petition process, from drafting and filing the document to serving notice on interested parties. You'll learn what to include, how to meet procedural requirements, and why proper formatting and legal content are equally important. By grasping these essentials now, you'll be better equipped to navigate the more detailed steps discussed in later chapters.

Understanding the Petition Process

A **petition** is the document that formally initiates a case in probate court. In estate and trust matters, a petition may be used to challenge a trust or will, request an accounting from a trustee or executor, seek the removal of a fiduciary, or request Letters of Administration when no executor was named. Filing a petition is necessary when court intervention is required to resolve an issue regarding an estate. If a will or trust is invalid due to lack of capacity, undue influence, fraud, or improper execution, the court must determine how the estate should be distributed. If an executor or trustee is failing in their duties, the court has the power to compel an accounting or remove them from their role. In cases where someone was wrongfully disinherited or assets are being mismanaged, filing a petition is often the only way to protect one's legal rights.

Once a petition is filed, the probate court plays a critical role in reviewing and ruling on the case. But it's important to understand that the court does not investigate on its own. It only evaluates the documents and arguments you present. This is why strong preparation is crucial. The court is responsible for ensuring that estate matters are handled fairly and in accordance with probate law. It reviews petitions for procedural compliance and legal sufficiency, ensures that all interested parties have been properly notified, and holds hearings where parties can present evidence and arguments. Ultimately, the court issues rulings that determine the outcome of the case. However, the court does not investigate claims on its own. It is up to the petitioner to provide evidence and construct a legally sound argument to justify their request.

Two Key Aspects of Your Petition

When drafting a petition, it is important to understand that the court will evaluate it based on two main factors: Procedural compliance and legal content. Both are equally important, as a petition that is legally strong but procedurally deficient may be rejected, and a petition that is perfectly formatted but lacks legal merit is unlikely to succeed.

Procedural compliance

Fefers to formatting and filing requirements that must be followed for the court to accept the petition. Many courts require petitions to be formatted on **pleading paper**, a type of paper that contains numbered lines designed to facilitate reference. Courts also impose rules regarding font size, spacing, and margin width, with most requiring petitions to be written in 12-point font, double-spaced, and properly structured with numbered paragraphs and section headings. Additionally, certain petitions require signatures to be in a specific format. Some courts accept electronic signatures through platforms like Adobe Sign, while others require wet signatures. Failure to meet these formatting and procedural requirements can result in delays or rejection of the petition.

Legal content

This portion of the petition is just as important as its procedural compliance. A strong petition must clearly state the legal basis for the request, provide a factual background explaining why court intervention is necessary, and present supporting evidence. It should be written in a way that is both persuasive and legally sound, citing relevant probate laws and statutes where applicable. The petition must also specify the relief sought, whether that is invalidating a trust, compelling an accounting, or removing an executor. Ultimately, a well-prepared petition combines both procedural compliance and strong legal arguments to give the court a clear and compelling basis to grant the requested relief.

To ensure that your petition is both accepted by the court and persuasive on its merits, it must meet the standards of procedural compliance and legal content, as shown in Table 7.1, *Procedural Compliance and Legal Content.*

Table 7.1. Procedural Compliance vs. Legal Content

Procedural Compliance	Legal Content
Proper formatting (12 pt, dbl. spaced)	Factual background and evidence
Court forms completed	Legal arguments/statues cited
Filing method followed	Relief clearly stated

Note. Successful petitions must satisfy both procedural and legal requirements. Procedural compliance ensures your document is accepted and processed by the court, while legal content gives the judge a valid reason to grant your request.

Key Steps to Filing a Petition

The filing process consists of several key steps, each of which must be completed correctly to ensure the petition is properly submitted and processed without unnecessary delays.

The first step is drafting the petition itself. This involves carefully structuring the document to meet all formatting and legal requirements. The petition should include a detailed factual background explaining the circumstances of the case, a summary of the legal grounds for the request, and a clear statement of the requested relief. Supporting documentation, such as financial records, medical documents, or witness declarations, should be included as exhibits where necessary.

Figure 7.1 below outlines the key steps involved in filing a petition, providing a visual guide to help petitioners navigate the process efficiently (see Figure 7.1, *Key Steps to Filing a Probate Petition*).

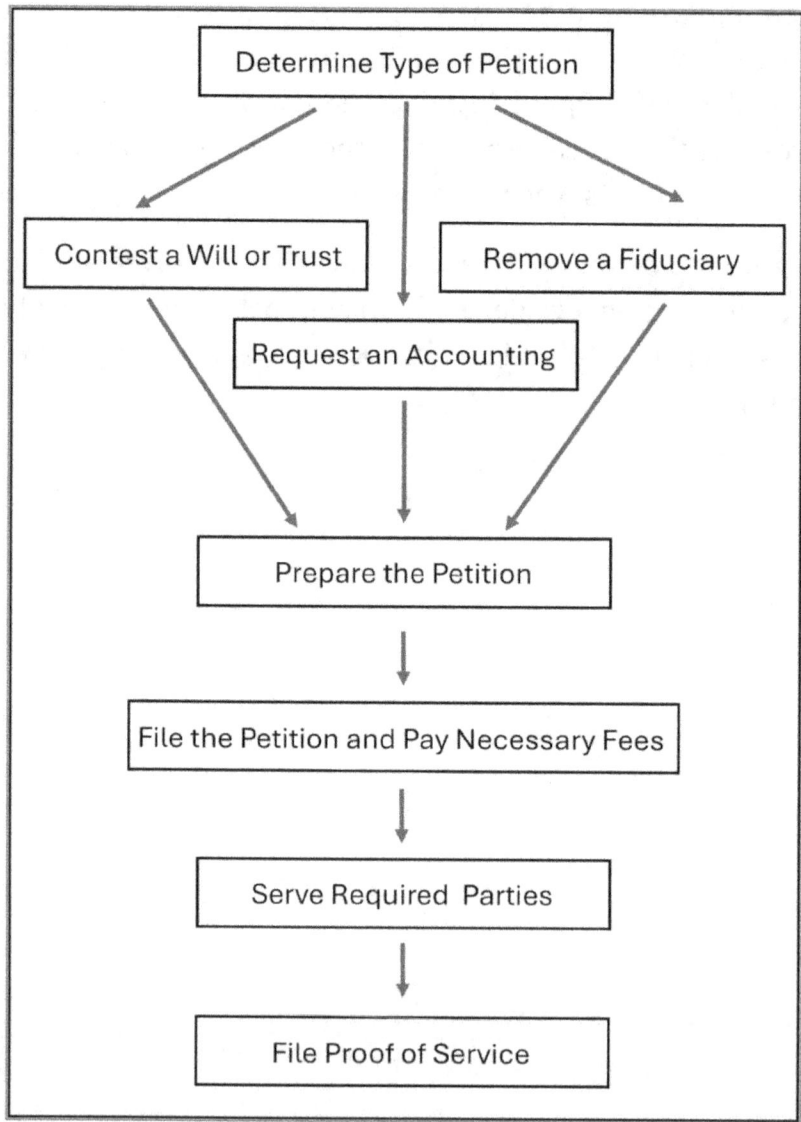

Figure 7.1. Key Steps to Filing a Probate Petition
Core steps in preparing and filing a petition in probate court. After determining the type of petition, petitioners must draft and file their petition, pay any required fees, serve notice to all required parties, and file proof of service.

After drafting the petition, the next step is completing any required court forms. Probate courts often require petitioners to submit additional forms alongside their petition, such as a case cover sheet, verification statements, and declarations. If the petitioner cannot afford the court filing fee, they may also need to submit a **fee waiver** request—a formal application asking the court to excuse payment based on financial hardship. Missing forms can lead to delays, so it is essential to check the specific filing requirements for the court where the petition is being filed.

Once the petition and required forms are complete, they must be submitted to the court. This step is known as **court filing**, which involved properly submitting legal documents following court rules. Some courts require electronic filing (e-filing), while others accept in-person or mail submissions. If filing in person, bring multiple copies to the court clerk's office to receive a file-stamped copy. For mail filing, use a tracked mailing service, such as USPS Certified Mail with Return Receipt, and include a pre-paid, self-addressed envelope for the court to return the filed copy. Upon submission, the petitioner will receive a case number, which must be used for tracking and future filings.

A filing fee is required at submission, and the amount varies by jurisdiction. Some courts accept online payments, while others require in-person or mailed payment. Petitioners who qualify for a fee waiver must submit the appropriate form along with the petition.

The final step is serving notice to all required parties and filing **proof of service**, a forma document confirming that notice has been properly given, with the court. The petitioner must notify all interested parties, such as beneficiaries, heirs, trustees, and executors. Depending on the case, service may involve personal delivery, certified mail, or publication in a newspaper if a party cannot be located. After serving notice, the petitioner must file a Proof of Service document to confirm that all required parties have been properly notified. Failure to serve notice correctly or file proof of service can result in delays or dismissal of the case.

Conclusion

Filing a petition is more than just filling out forms. It requires careful planning, attention to detail, and a clear presentation of legal arguments. Ensuring both procedural compliance and strong legal content increases the chances of the court accepting your petition and addressing your claims. While the process may seem complex, breaking it into manageable steps makes it more approachable. The next chapters will delve deeper into each stage of the filing process, providing practical tips and examples to guide you through the paperwork and court procedures.

Figure 7.2 highlights the key takeaways of the most important aspects of filing a petition in probate court, helping you avoid common pitfalls and prepare for a successful submission (see Figure 7.2, *Key Takeaways – Filing Process*).

1. A petition formally starts a probate case. It outlines the claims, legal grounds, and relief sought, allowing the court to address disputes over a trust, will, or fiduciary actions.
2. Procedural compliance and strong legal content are essential. Proper formatting, clear legal arguments, and supporting evidence increase the chances of acceptance.
3. Common reasons to file include contesting a trust or will, requesting an accounting, or removing a fiduciary. The petition must clearly explain why court intervention is needed.
4. Include a clear factual background, stated legal grounds, and the specific relief requested. Citing relevant statutes and attaching exhibits strengthen the case.
5. Complete required court forms and pay the filing fee. Check local court rules for e-filing requirements and submission methods.
6. Serve notice to all interested parties and file proof of service. Use the correct service method—personal delivery, certified mail, or publication, depending on what the law allows.
7. Track the case using the assigned case number, and reference it in all future filings.
8. Common mistakes include formatting errors or incomplete documents. Careful preparation and following court rules help prevent delays or rejections.

Figure 7.2. Key Takeaways – Filing Process
Summarizes key steps for filing a probate petition, such as completing forms, meeting procedural requirements, and serving notice. Following court rules and submitting strong legal content helps avoid delays, rejections, and common filing mistakes.

CHAPTER 8

Legal Content of the Petition

Introduction

Drafting a strong and effective probate petition requires more than just presenting grievances. It demands a structured legal argument rooted in statutory law, case law, and factual evidence. In the legal process, petitions are not merely storytelling devices; they are formal requests that must clearly articulate legal claims, cite relevant statutes, and present credible support.

Filing a petition isn't just about bringing your case before the court. It's about making a compelling, legally sound argument. The petition itself must be clear, precise, and well-supported, as the court's initial focus is often on procedural compliance. This includes ensuring that the petition is properly formatted, that all necessary parties have been notified, and that the legal request and cited code sections are accurate and complete. If any element is missing or ambiguous, procedural notes may be issued, or the hearing may be delayed. Meeting these requirements allows the case to move forward, potentially involving settlement conferences, discovery deadlines, or future hearings.

This chapter guides you through the essential legal elements of a probate petition. You'll learn how to use California law to strengthen your claims, understand core legal terms like statutes, probate codes, and case law, and apply practical writing tips to create a clear, credible petition.

Start Here: Petition Builder Worksheet
Before you begin drafting your petition, use the **Petition Builder Worksheet** to map out the key facts, legal grounds, and relief you're requesting. Think of it as your legal outline—it helps you organize your thoughts, clarify your claims, and get ready to write clearly and confidently.

> **Draft Your Story.** Start with the **Petition Builder Worksheet** to put your story together. Download it at https://properprobate.guide/california-filing or scan  the QR code. It is designed to help you organize your petition with fill-in-the-blank prompts and build a stronger filing package.

Essential Legal Elements of a Petition

Title and Relief Sought

Every petition begins with a title. This is one of the most important sentences in your entire document. It frames your request and sets the tone for what the court is being asked to consider.

A strong title should include three key parts:

1. What you are submitting (for example, a Petition, Objection, or Motion)
2. What you want the court to do (this is called the "relief sought")
3. Why you want it (the legal reason, such as lack of capacity, undue influence, or financial elder abuse)

Example:

Petition to Invalidate the March 5, 2025, Amendment to the Jane Doe Living Trust Based on Undue Influence and Lack of Capacity

This title includes all three elements:

1. You are submitting a **Petition.**
2. You are asking the court to **Invalidate** a specific document.
3. You are explaining that the legal basis is **Undue Influence** and **Lack of Capacity**.

This structure clearly identifies the core issue of your case. It applies not just to petitions, but to any document asking the court to take action, such as a motion, objection, or supplement. In short, your title should state: what it is, what you want, and why the law supports it (see Figure 8.1, *Examples of Clear and Effective Court Titles*).

Be specific and direct. Avoid vague or emotional titles like "Petition for Justice" or "To Make Things Right." While those may express how you feel, they don't tell the court what legal action you're requesting or why the court has the authority to grant it. A clear, neutral title shows the judge that you understand your request and the legal framework behind it.

- *Petition* to **Invalidate the 2020 Amendment to the Smith Family Trust** for Lack of Capacity
- *Petition* to **Remove John Doe as Trustee** Due to Breach of Fiduciary Duty
- *Petition* to **Compel Accounting of Trust Assets** Pursuant to Probate Code § 17200
- *Motion* to **Compel Accounting of Estate Assets**
- *Supplement* to **Address Probate Notes Filed May 12, 2025**
- *Objection* to **Petition for Probate** Due to Suspected Undue Influence

Figure 8.1. Examples of Clear and Effective Court Titles
*How to format court filing titles using three elements: (1) **type of document** (italicized), (2) **action requested** (bolded), and (3) **legal reason or statute** (underlined). Not all filings need a legal citation, but it helps when requesting major actions like removing a trustee or invalidating a trust.*

Introduction

The introduction sets the stage for your petition. It identifies who you are, your relationship to the **decedent** (the person who passed away) or **settlor** (if the person is still alive), the legal document being challenged (such as a living trust, amended trust, or will), and a brief summary of your legal claim. When applicable, identify the respondent—the person whose actions or role are being challenged. Keep the tone factual, concise, and neutral.

Example:

Petitioners JOHN DOE and MARY DOE SMITH ("PETITIONERS"), individuals and biological children of JANE DOE ("DECEDENT"), hereby respectfully submit this Petition to Invalidate the March 5, 2025, Amendment to the Jane Doe Living Trust based on Undue Influence and Lack of Capacity (the "AMENDMENT"). The AMENDMENT was allegedly executed at a time when the Decedent lacked testamentary capacity and was under the influence of Respondent JOHN DOE, her nephew and caretaker at the time.

Jurisdiction, Venue, and Standing

This section is often short, usually just one or two sentences per heading, but it's important. The court must know three things:

1. that it has authority to hear your case.
2. that it's being filed in the right place.
3. that you're the right person to file it.

Jurisdiction

Jurisdiction refers to the type of case the court has the authority to hear. Since this is a probate matter involving a trust, will, estate, or conservatorship, it falls under the jurisdiction of the California Superior Court, Probate Division. Probate matters are state-level issues governed by the California Probate Code.

Venue

Venue refers to the appropriate county within the state to file your case. In California, venue is typically proper in the county where the decedent lived at the time of death or where the estate or trust is administered.

Example

"Venue is proper in Los Angeles County because the decedent resided, and the trust assets are located in Los Angeles."

Standing

Standing means that you have a legal right to bring the petition. California Probate Code § 48 defines an "interested person" as someone with a financial or legal interest in the outcome. This can include:

- Named beneficiaries
- Heirs under intestate succession
- Prior beneficiaries who were later disinherited
- Creditors of the estate.

Even if you were disinherited under a contested amendment, you may still have standing to challenge that amendment because if it is found to be invalidated, your interest could be restored. At this stage, you don't need to prove your entire case. You only need to show that you have a potential legal interest if your claims succeed.

Example:

"Petitioner has standing under Probate Code § 48 as an interested person, being the decedent's child and a beneficiary under the original trust."

Our Experience

In our own case, we were not named in a prior trust or will—at least not in any version we had access to. We were the biological children of the decedent and filed a petition to invalidate both the trust and its amendment. At one point, the court asked who would inherit if the trust were invalidated. We explained that if the trust was voided and no valid will existed, the estate should be treated under California's intestate succession laws, as if no trust or will had existed, meaning the estate would be divided equally among the decedent's children.

Factual Background / Statement of Facts

Before presenting your legal arguments, it's essential to establish the factual background of your case by explaining what happened, when it happened, and how those events led to the petition. The statement of facts serves as the foundation for your legal claims. It should be written in plain language, free of legal conclusions, and follow a clear chronological order.

In the sections that follow, we will examine the most common legal reasons for challenging a living trust or will. For each, you'll learn the relevant law, the types of evidence that support the claim, and how courts have interpreted similar situations. We'll also provide sample language to help you structure your arguments.

This is where your personal knowledge and the law intersect. It's not just about recounting events; it's about demonstrating how those events may constitute legal wrongdoing. The factual background should include relevant dates, relationships, interactions, and key events that led to filing the petition.

Start by briefly describing the decedent's life circumstances leading up to the creation of the trust or will. Include information about their mental and physical health, living situation, changes in family dynamics, and who was involved in their care. Then, outline the sequence of events related to the trust or will including when and how it was created, amended, or challenged, and by whom. To help organize your thoughts, consider using a timeline (see Table 8.1, *Sample Timeline of Events*), followed by a narrative of the events (see Figure 8.2, *Written Narrative of Key Events*).

Table 8.1. Sample Timeline of Events

Date	Event	Notes
01/15/18	Diagnosed with early-stage Alzheimer's disease	Mild cognitive impairment noted in medical records
06/22/18	Cognitive decline on annual physical	Reports of confusion, forgetfulness
09/10/18	New trust named caregiver sole beneficiary	Adult children not informed
09/14/18	Hospitalized for UTI and confusion	Four days after trust execution
10/02/18	Second hospitalization for dehydration, fall	Discharge notes – memory impairment
11/01/18	Neuro. assessment: MMSE score of 18/30	Cognitive impairment documented
12/05/18	Psychiatric treatment for depression, anxiety	Social withdrawal and dependency
02/10/19	Caregiver assumed full financial control	Began managing accounts and bills

Note. This fictionalized timeline is based on a real case. It shows how factual background can be presented in clear, chronological order without including legal conclusions.

II. FACTUAL BACKGROUND

5. JANE DOE ("DECEDENT") was born on [DATE] and passed away on [DATE].

6. Prior to her death, DECEDENT executed various estate planning documents, including the Living Trust dated September 10, 2018 ("TRUST"), which is the subject of this Petition.

7. At the time the TRUST was executed, DECEDENT was experiencing significant cognitive decline, as documented in her medical records, including a diagnosis of early-stage Alzheimer's disease in January 2018 and subsequent deterioration throughout 2018.

8. In June 2018, DECEDENT's primary care physician documented increasing confusion, forgetfulness, and difficulty managing daily activities.

9. Despite her cognitive decline, DECEDENT executed the TRUST naming her caregiver, JOHN SMITH ("RESPONDENT"), as the sole beneficiary, without informing her adult children or other close family members.

10. Just four days after executing the TRUST, DECEDENT was hospitalized for a urinary tract infection, dehydration, and documented episodes of acute confusion.

11. DECEDENT was again hospitalized in October 2018 following a fall at her residence, where medical discharge notes recorded moderate memory impairment and disorientation.

12. On November 1, 2018, a neurological evaluation administered a Mini Mental Status Examination (MMSE) in which DECEDENT scored 18 out of 30, indicating moderate cognitive impairment.

13. In December 2018, DECEDENT began psychiatric treatment for depression, anxiety, and social withdrawal, further evidencing her vulnerability and declining mental health.

14. By February 2019, RESPONDENT had assumed control over DECEDENT's financial affairs, including managing her bank accounts and making financial decisions on her behalf.

PETITION TO INVALIDATE A LIVING TRUST BASED ON LACK OF CAPACITY AND UNDUE INFLUENCE

Figure 8.2. Written Narrative of Key Events
How to present a factual background section in a probate petition. It uses a numbered paragraph format on California pleading paper and is based on a fictionalized real case. The narrative clearly outlines relevant facts in chronological order without drawing legal conclusions.

Avoid drawing legal conclusions in this section. Focus solely on presenting the facts in a clear and neutral manner.

Note to Reader

If the timeline or sample statement you just read feels strong, I want you to know—it may not have started that way.

When I first filed, all I had was an unused mother-daughter plane ticket for a trip my mom was too sick to take, a doctor's note showing she needed caretaker assistance, and a photo of me visiting her in the hospital.

A lot of what we knew came from witness accounts—family members who shared what they saw and remembered. We didn't submit formal declarations at first. We just told the story the best we could with what we had.

Most of what I later used—medical records, dates, etc.—came months or years later after a lot of digging.

Don't wait until you have everything to start. Start with the pieces you do have. Sometimes, that's all you need to get started

What is Statutory Law?

Statutory law consists of written laws passed by the state legislature. In probate cases, this typically includes the California Probate Code, as well as related laws from the Welfare & Institutions Code **or** Civil Code. These statutes establish rules for matters like trust creation, trustee duties, and conduct that may constitute financial elder abuse or undue influence.

If you are representing yourself, citing even one or two relevant codes can demonstrate that your petition is well-researched and legally grounded.

The California Probate Code was established to ensure consistency and clarity in handling estates, trusts, and related legal matters. Legislators pass these laws, which are then organized by subject and assigned section numbers. Including these references in your petition shows how the law supports your claim.

How to Access Statutory Law

You can find California's official laws and codes at the California Legislative Information website: https://leginfo.legislature.ca.gov. From the homepage, click on "California Law" in the top menu to view all the state's legal codes.

- To access probate-related statutes, select the Probate Code, which covers wills, trusts, and estate administration.
- For conservatorships, mental health, and some public services, choose the Welfare and Institutions Code.

The website is user-friendly, providing the full text of each code section along with search and browsing tools to help you find current laws.

Common Probate Code Sections

The following are some of the most commonly cited California code sections in contested probate cases, including trust disputes and elder abuse claims (see Table 8.2, *Commonly Cited*

California Statutory Codes). These provide a starting point for understanding how legal issues are framed. A full reference list with additional sections is available in the appendix.

Table 8.2. Commonly Cited California Statutory Codes

Legal Issue	Legal Issue
Lack of Capacity	Probate Code §§ 810–812 – Presumption of capacity and mental functioning standards
Undue Influence	Welfare & Institutions Code § 15610.70 – Definition and indicators of undue influence
Breach of Fiduciary Duty	Probate Code §§ 16000–16015 – Trustee duties; §§ 16400–16460 – Breach and remedies
Financial Elder Abuse	Welfare & Institutions Code § 15610.30 – Taking or assisting in the taking of assets
Faud	Civil Code §§ 1572, 3294 – Actual fraud and malice for punitive damages
Trust Contests	Probate Code §§ 850, 17200, 16061.7 – Petition authority, notice, and trust administration
Notice & Filing Deadlines	Probate Code §§ 850, 16061.7, 17200, 11704 – Timing for trust disputes and required filings

Note. A quick-reference list of California codes often used in probate and trust litigation.

Statutory law tells you *what* the rule is. If your claim is based on *breach of fiduciary duty*, you might cite a statute that outlines a trustee's responsibilities. If your claim is based on *elder abuse*, you would cite the statute that defines it and explains what behavior qualifies. You don't need to quote entire sections. Simply reference the right code and explaining it in plain language is enough.

The goal is to help the judge understand how the facts of your case line up with the rules written in law. Here's how to connect the dots.

In court, you want to tell your story, backed by evidence, to demonstrate how the rule was broken. You can use this simple structure to explain your case:

1. Describe what happened (the facts)
2. explain why it matters (the harm or wrongdoing)
3. name the rule that applies (statutory support).

Examples

Example #1: Breach of Fiduciary Duty

1. The last full accounting was over two years ago. Trustee has refused to respond to written requests, did not disclose proceeds from property sales, and did not pay property taxes.
2. Mismanagement and neglect
3. Probate code § 16000

Putting it All together:

"The last full accounting was provided over two years ago. Since then, the trustee has refused to respond to written requests, failed to disclose proceeds from property sales, and allowed trust-owned real estate taxes to become delinquent. These actions show a pattern of mismanagement and neglect. This is a breach of fiduciary duty under *Probate Code § 16000*, which requires the trustee to act in the best interests of the beneficiaries."

Example #2:: Financial Elder Abuse

1. Our mother was isolated from family. The respondent would not let us speak to her on the phone. Convinced to sign over her home despite memory loss.
2. Financial elder abuse
3. Welfare and Institute Code §15610.30

Putting it All together:

"In the final months of our mother's life, the respondent isolated her from family, restricted phone calls, and convinced her to sign over her home even though she had documented memory loss and confusion. This conduct falls under the definition of financial elder abuse in Welfare and Institutions Code § 15610.30, which includes taking property from someone over 65 through undue influence or deception."

Example #3: Undue Influence

1. Two months before our father passed, a new trust amendment was signed that disinherited five of six

children. The caretaker inherited everything. At the time, our father had been diagnosed with dementia.
2. Undue Influence
3. Welfare and Institute Code §15610.70

Putting it All together:

"Two months before my father passed, a new trust amendment was created that disinherited five of his six children and left everything to the caregiver. At the time, my father had been diagnosed with moderate dementia and had lost the ability to understand financial decisions. This raises serious concerns about undue influence as defined in Welfare and Institutions Code § 15610.70, which includes factors like isolation, dependency, and unfair outcomes."

These examples show how your personal experience can be expressed using legal terms, grounded in specific statutes like the Probate Code or Welfare and Institutions Code. Next, we'll explore how past legal decisions, called case law, can support your argument by illustrating how courts have interpreted these laws in similar disputes.

Once you understand what the law says, whether it's the Probate Code or the Welfare & Institutions Code, the next question is: how have courts applied it in real life? That's where case law comes in.

What is Case Law?

Case law refers to published decisions from California appellate courts or the California Supreme Court that interpret and apply statutes in real-life situations. These decisions carry legal authority and can be cited to support your petition. While Probate Code sections tell you the rules, case law shows how judges have interpreted those rules when disputes arise.

Example: Estate of Heggstad (1993)

One significant California appellate case related to trust asset inclusion is *Estate of Heggstad (1993) 16 Cal.App.4th 943.* This case established that a written declaration of trust by the owner of real property is sufficient to include that property in the trust estate, even if the title was not formally transferred through a deed.

In *Heggstad*, Halvard L. Heggstad created a revocable living trust and included a schedule listing his real properties. However, he did not execute a deed to formally transfer one of the properties, an interest in real estate, into the trust. When Halvard passed away, his son, Glen Heggstad, acting as successor trustee, filed a *Heggstad petition* to confirm that the property listed on the trust schedule was part of the trust, despite the absence of a recorded deed.

The probate court ruled in favor of Glen, and the California Court of Appeal upheld the decision. The court found that a *Heggstad petition* (under *Probate Code § 850)* could be used to confirm that assets listed in the trust schedule are part of the trust estate. The ruling clarified that the written intent of the settlor, as expressed in the trust document, is sufficient to include the asset, even without formal title transfer.

How Case Law Affects Your Petition

In California, probate cases are first heard in the Superior Court, Probate Division. If someone disagrees with the ruling, they can appeal the decision to the California Court of Appeal. In rare cases, the issue may go even higher, to the California Supreme Court, which reviews only selected cases that raise significant legal questions. When appellate or supreme courts issue rulings, those decisions become case law and are binding on all lower courts.

Citing relevant case law in your petition can strengthen your position, as it demonstrates that your legal argument has been recognized in higher courts.

Our Experience

After receiving a preliminary financial accounting, we noticed that several assets listed in Schedule A of our mother's trust, such as stocks, bonds, IRAs, vacant land, and limited partnerships, were not included in the accounting. At that point, we considered filing a *Heggstad petition* under Probate Code § 850 to confirm that these assets were part of the trust. Since the trust document itself listed these assets, the petition would seek a court order recognizing them as part of the trust estate, even though the formal title transfer was not completed.

Putting It All Together – Sample Argument Paragraph

Here's how to combine facts, harm, and law into a single, persuasive paragraph.

1. **What happened**: The March 2020 trust amendment was signed after the decedent was diagnosed with moderate dementia in December 2019 (Exhibit A). Caregiver declarations (Exhibit B) describe frequent confusion, memory lapses, and inability to manage daily tasks.
2. **Why it matters**: These facts indicate that the decedent lacked the cognitive ability to understand and approve significant legal changes, raising serious concerns about mental capacity at the time the amendment was executed.
3. **What rule applies**: Under *Probate Code §§ 810–812*, a person must understand the nature and consequences of their decisions. In *Andersen v. Hunt* (2011), the court invalidated a trust based on similar signs of incapacity.

Sample Argument

"The March 2020 trust amendment should be invalidated due to lack of capacity. According to her medical records, the decedent was diagnosed with moderate dementia in December 2019 (Exhibit A). Caregiver declarations (Exhibit B) describe frequent confusion, memory lapses, and inability to manage daily tasks. Under Probate Code §§ 810–812, a person must understand the nature and consequences of their decisions. In *Andersen v. Hunt* (2011), the court found a trust invalid where the decedent had similar cognitive impairments."

Prayer for/Requested Relief

In some court documents, this section may be labeled **"Prayer for Relief."** That's just traditional legal language meaning: *"Here's what I'm asking the court to do."* In this guide, we use the more modern and descriptive phrase: **Requested Relief.** Whether you see *prayer, relief sought,* or *requested orders,* they all mean the same thing: this is where you tell the court exactly what outcome you want.

This is where you formally state what you're asking the court to do. Your requests should flow naturally from the facts you presented and the legal claims you made in your petition.

While your petition title may introduce the core issue, such as asking the court to invalidate a trust or amendment, the Requested Relief section allows you to clearly spell out everything you want the court to do in response.

Example:

Petitioner respectfully requests that the Court:

1. Invalidate the March 5, 2025, Amendment to the Jane Doe Living Trust on the grounds of lack of capacity and undue influence.
2. Remove John Doe as acting trustee due to breach of fiduciary duty.
3. Order a full and complete accounting of all trust assets and transactions.
4. Return any wrongfully obtained assets to the trust for proper distribution.

Each point should be clear and specific. Avoid vague or emotional language. This section is not about restating your grievances. It's about clearly outlining the legal outcomes you're asking the court to order.

Supporting Evidence

While evidence is crucial to your petition, it's important to know that you are not typically required to submit all your supporting exhibits when you file your initial petition. The initial filing is your chance to present the basic facts, identify the legal wrongs, and explain why the court has the authority to intervene. Most of the detailed documentation, such as medical records, financial transactions, and witness declarations, is usually saved for the discovery phase or later hearings.

Essential Documents to Include

That said, there are certain documents that should be attached to your petition. These usually include the document you are challenging (such as the living trust, will, or an amendment), and any other legal documents that are directly referenced in your petition, such as a prior version of a trust, certification of trust, or notice of trustee duties

(Note, "Notice of trustee duties" is only relevant if the trust is already being administered).

If you already have a strong piece of evidence, such as a declaration from a caregiver or a particularly telling email, you can choose to attach it with your petition. If you do, make sure to label it clearly as an exhibit: Exhibit A, Exhibit B, etc., and refer to it in the body of your petition. But if you're still collecting documentation or plan to introduce evidence later, that's okay too. The court does not expect your petition to include every shred of proof upfront.

Common documents to attach to your petition

- A copy of the trust, will, or amendment being contested
- A prior version of the trust (if available)
- Notice of Trust Administration (for a trust)
- Notice of Petition to Administer Estate (for a will)
- Key evidence, such as medical records, witness declarations, or financial documents, can be submitted later or introduced during hearings.

Guidelines for Including Exhibits

1. Label each document as an exhibit (e.g., Exhibit A, Exhibit B)
2. Provide a clear, descriptive title (e.g., Exhibit A: Geriatric Evaluation)
3. Reference the exhibit clearly in your writing (e.g., "See Exhibit A: Geriatric Evaluation")
4. Avoid attaching documents that aren't directly relevant to your claims

You can also preserve evidence by saving important emails or text message threads as PDFs or screenshots. These may not go in the petition itself but can be powerful later. In short: include what's necessary to show the court what the petition is about, but don't feel pressured to prove your entire case at this stage. That's what discovery and hearings are for.

By structuring your petition carefully and grounding each section in law and evidence, you show the court that your case is serious and supported. This isn't about emotional appeals. It's about legal persuasion.

Final Tips for Drafting a Persuasive Petition

A well-prepared petition is more than just a formality. It lays the groundwork for your entire probate case. To make your petition persuasive and effective, follow these key principles:

- **Clarity and Conciseness:** State allegations and arguments clearly, without unnecessary length. Avoid vague or overly detailed points. Each claim should be easy to follow.
- **Grounded in Law:** Base your arguments in probate law. Reference relevant codes, statutes, and case law to demonstrate legal authority rather than just expressing personal grievances.
- **Evidence-Driven Assertions:** You don't need all evidence up front but structure your claims to show they are based on facts. Mention the types of evidence you will use later.
- **Tell a Compelling Legal Story:** Present your narrative clearly, aligning facts with legal principles. Show that your claims are credible and based on evidence, even if not all documents are submitted.

- **Avoid Redundancy:** Don't repeat evidence or arguments. Refer back to where information was first introduced (e.g., "See Section II.A regarding medical history").

By keeping your petition clear, legally sound, and well-organized, you increase your chances of achieving a favorable outcome. Approach your drafting process with the mindset that every word matters. Your petition is your voice in the courtroom.

Avoid These Common Mistakes in Probate Petitions

Filing a probate petition can be a complex and emotional process. Whether you're a self-represented litigant or a legal professional preparing a petition, avoiding common mistakes is essential to presenting a strong and persuasive case. Here are some of the most frequent errors that can lead to delays, challenges, or even dismissal, along with practical guidance on how to avoid them.

- **Vague statements without supporting evidence.** One of the most common mistakes in probate petitions is failing to include enough factual detail or documentation. Courts rely on specific, verifiable information to evaluate claims. Simply stating that "the will is invalid" or "the property should go to me" without explanation or proof won't be enough. Instead, ensure that every key statement in your petition is supported by facts and evidence, such as a copy of a will, bank records, emails, or witness declarations. Be specific. Who did what? When? Where? How?

- **Relying on feelings instead of facts and law.** Probate cases often involve grief, family conflict, and deep emotions, but courts do not decide cases based on what feels fair. Saying "This isn't right" or "It's not fair" is not a legal argument. The court must follow the law, not personal sentiment. Focus on objective facts and relevant legal principles. Explain why the outcome you're asking for is supported by law—not just why it feels unjust.
- **Making unsupported legal claims.** It's not enough to state a grievance. You must show how the law applies to your situation. A petition that fails to cite relevant legal authority (such as statutes or case law) may be dismissed or ignored. Reference the specific sections of the Probate Code or other statutes that apply. If possible, include citations to court decisions that support your position. This shows the court that your petition is grounded in legal reasoning, not just personal opinion.
- **Failing to clearly state the relief requested.** Another frequent oversight is not clearly telling the court what you want it to do. If your petition doesn't spell out the relief you're seeking, the court may delay the case or deny the request altogether. State your requested relief clearly at both the beginning and the end of the petition. If you're asking for multiple things (e.g., invalidate a trust, remove a trustee, compel an accounting), list each item clearly and specifically so the court understands what you're requesting.
- **Assuming the judge already knows the facts.** Another common mistake is writing the petition as if the judge already understands the full story. Judges hear

dozens of cases and don't know your family dynamics, the history behind a will, or why something matters unless you explain it clearly. Spell out the relevant facts with clarity but stay focused. Include necessary background information but avoid unnecessary detail or repetition. The court only knows what you write in the petition. So write like you're introducing the story for the first time.

- **Not reusing relevant evidence across legal theories.** In many cases, a single piece of evidence may support multiple legal arguments. For example, evidence of a person's declining medical condition might support both a claim of vulnerability and a claim of lack of capacity. A common mistake is either repeating the same facts unnecessarily to organize your arguments, support them with relevant documents when needed, and be specific about what you want the court to do. Avoid relying on emotion or vague claims. Instead, let the law and your clarity speak for you.

By addressing common mistakes and following the key principles outlined, you create a petition that is not just technically accurate but also persuasive and credible. This structured, evidence-based approach will significantly increase your chances of success in probate proceedings.

Conclusion

A well-drafted probate petition is more than just a formality. It's a foundational document that sets the stage for your entire case. By combining clear, legally sound arguments with relevant factual support, you demonstrate to the court that your petition deserves serious consideration. Applying the strategies and principles outlined in this chapter will help ensure that your petition is not only legally persuasive but also procedurally compliant, increasing your chances of success in probate proceedings.

Figure 8.3 outlines the key takeaways for the legal content of the petition (see Figure 8.3, *Legal Content*).

1. A strong petition should clearly state the title and relief sought, establish jurisdiction and standing, present a factual background, outline legal grounds and arguments, and include any necessary supporting documents.
2. Allegations should be concise, organized, and free from unnecessary complexity.
3. Citing relevant probate laws and case precedents strengthens your argument and shows the court that your petition is grounded in law.
4. Evidence matters—even if it's not submitted all at once. Claims should be supported by medical records, financial statements, or witness declarations when appropriate.
5. Common mistakes include vague claims, missing legal references, emotional reasoning, and not clearly stating the relief requested.

Figure 8.3. Key Takeaways – Legal Content
Outlines the core elements of a strong petition—clarity, legal support, and evidence. Also flags common mistakes like vague claims and emotional reasoning.

If your story is real, your evidence strong, and your writing clear, your petition becomes your voice in the courtroom—even before you ever set foot inside.

CHAPTER 9

Legal Grounds for Contesting a Trust or Will

Introduction

When challenging a trust or will in probate court, it's not enough to simply feel that something was unfair. You need to demonstrate that a legal rule was violated. Without clear legal grounds, your petition could be dismissed before it even begins. This chapter breaks down the most common legal claims you can use to challenge a trust or will, helping you translate your concerns into actionable legal arguments.

We'll explore the most common legal grounds for contesting a trust or will, including lack of capacity, undue influence, financial elder abuse, and breach of fiduciary duty. Understanding these causes of action and how to properly assert them will help you build a strong, legally grounded petition.

Before You Begin: Start Gathering Evidence

To support any legal claim, you'll need more than a strong narrative—you'll need proof. Use the **Evidence Checklist** to start identifying documents, records, and witness statements that can support your case.

> **Build Your Evidence.** Use the **Evidence Checklist** to start gathering what you'll need. Download it at  [https://l.ead.me/bg3fqW] or scan the QR code. It walks you through collecting the proof you'll need to strengthen your case.

Legal Claims / Causes of Action

A cause of action is a specific legal reason why you're asking the court to step in. It's not just that something unfair happened. It's that the law was violated, and you're asking the court to fix it. A complaint without legal backing doesn't go far. The court doesn't decide who's right or wrong based on feelings. It decides based on law. In other words, a cause of action is your story, translated into legal terms the court can act on. Each cause of action is like a building block in your petition. The more clearly and completely you present each one, the stronger your overall case.

> **Disclaimer:** Before we dive into specific legal claims like undue influence or lack of capacity, I want to be clear: this guide is educational. I'm not a lawyer, and I'm not giving you legal advice. What I share here is based on public information, my own experience, and what I've learned along the way. If you're unsure how these laws apply to your situation, talk to a licensed attorney.

Before diving into the specific legal claims, a quick reminder. What I share here is based on publicly available legal information, my own lived experience, and what I've learned through research and trial by fire. It's meant to guide and empower—but it's not a substitute for professional legal advice.

> **Do I Need Every Cause of Action?** No. You don't need to allege every possible cause of action. If even one of them is strong and supported by evidence, that may be enough to move your case forward. The goal isn't to list everything-it's to focus on what you can prove. Filing weak or unsupported claims can make your petition harder to take seriously, so choose the ones that best match your facts.

In probate court, common causes of action include lack of capacity, undue influence, financial elder abuse, and breach of fiduciary duty. In this section, we'll break them down one at a time explaining what each claim means, what the law says, what kind of evidence supports it, and how to explain it in your petition. This will help you build the legal backbone of your case.

Cause of Action I: Lack of Capacity

Lack of capacity means the decedent did not understand what they were signing, what it meant, or how it would affect the distribution of their assets and the people in their life. Someone with capacity should understand things like who their children, spouse, or close relatives are; who they're leaving things to and who they're not; and how their choices will affect those people emotionally or financially.

Legal Standard for Capacity

Under *Probate Code § 810*, adults are generally presumed to have capacity. However, *Probate Code §§ 811 and 812* lay out the specific impairments and decision-making deficiencies that may rebut that presumption, such as memory loss, delusions, or inability to understand the consequences of a decision (see Table 9.1, *How California Probate Code Defines Mental Capacity*). These laws apply to a wide range of legal acts, including the execution of a trust or will.

Table 9.1. How California Probate Code Defines Mental Capacity

Probate Code	What is Says
§ 810	Everyone is presumed to have capacity unless shown otherwise.
§ 811	The court looks for impairments like memory loss, confusion, or delusions.
§ 812	A person lacks capacity if they don't understand, appreciate, or communicate a decision.

Full text available at leginfo.legislature.ca.gov

Note: This table summarizes the key sections of California Probate Code that govern whether someone had the mental capacity to sign a legal document. These rules are often cited in probate petitions involving lack of capacity.

Proving lack of capacity at the time a trust or will was executed can be challenging. Capacity may fluctuate, and the person may not recognize or admit their decline. They typically won't say things like **"I'm confused"** or **"I don't understand."** In fact, people experiencing early cognitive decline often try to appear normal and hide their confusion—especially when they're scared or in denial. That's what makes capacity so hard to evaluate after the fact.

Direct evidence, such as a doctor declaring someone incompetent at the exact time they signed a document, is rare. Most cases rely on circumstantial evidence: patterns in medical records, observations of unusual behavior, memory issues, or testimony from those close to the decedent. The court looks at the whole picture, not just isolated moments. A lack of capacity claim becomes especially compelling when the document in question significantly alters long-standing estate plans or removes expected beneficiaries.

Building Your Case: Evidence for Lack of Capacity

This cause of action argues that the decedent lacked mental capacity at the time the document was created or amended. Common signs of incapacity include a diagnosis of Alzheimer's, dementia, or another condition affecting cognition. Frequent confusion or forgetfulness, an inability to recognize close family members or manage finances, and significant changes to long-standing estate plans or the removal of expected beneficiaries are also indicators.

To support your claim, include evidence such as medical records documenting cognitive impairment, statements from caregivers or family describing unusual behavior, expert opinions from physicians or geriatric specialists, and a timeline showing when the trust or will was executed in relation to a diagnosis or noticeable decline.

> ## Our Experience: Facing Skepticism Despite Evidence
>
> In our case, we gathered both circumstantial and direct evidence. My mother was diagnosed with end-stage kidney disease just one month before executing her living trust. We obtained a doctor's note that stated she required caretaker assistance four months before signing the trust. Ironically, the caretaker later became the sole beneficiary.
>
> Three days after signing the trust, my mother was hospitalized. Ten days later, she was admitted again for two full weeks. Medical records from these visits noted memory loss, anxiety, and depression. A month later, she was treated for cognitive issues. Two months after that, the respondent himself told medical staff that my mother had been experiencing memory problems for the past year and had perseveration for the past three years—repeating the same story at length and boasting without noticing others' reactions.
>
> Despite this comprehensive evidence, I frequently heard comments like, "These cases are hard to prove," or "I'm not sure your case is strong enough." It was frustrating. I had gathered every possible document and witness statement, but it still didn't seem to be enough.
>
> At our Mandatory Settlement Conference, the Commissioner mentioned that the opposing attorney only needed to "create an issue of fact" to undermine my case. Whether that was

> meant to encourage settlement or simply to offer a reality check, it was unsettling.
>
> Still, I held on to what I knew: the truth of her condition, the thorough documentation we had gathered, and the inconsistencies in the opposing side's claims. These moments can be tough and can shake your confidence, but they do not mean your case isn't worth pursuing. Trust in the truth and keep pushing forward.

Cause of Action II: Undue Influence

Undue influence occurs when someone exerts excessive pressure on a vulnerable person to change their trust or will in a way that benefits the influencer rather than reflecting the true wishes of the decedent. This type of manipulation often happens behind closed doors and without witnesses. The influencer doesn't openly declare their intent to manipulate; instead, it shows up in patterns of behavior, secret meetings, isolation from family, or sudden and dramatic changes to legal documents.

As with lack of capacity, direct evidence of undue influence is rare. Most claims rely on circumstantial evidence—clues that, when taken together, point to improper persuasion.

Legal Standard for Undue Influence

Courts commonly apply the four-factor test from *Estate of Sarabia* (1990) 221 Cal.App.3d 599 to determine whether undue influence occurred. These factors are:

1. Vulnerability of the victim,

2. Apparent authority of the influencer,
3. Actions or tactics used to exert influence, and
4. Inequity of the result.

Vulnerability of the Victim

This first factor focuses entirely on the condition of the decedent—their physical, mental, or emotional state at the time the legal document was created or amended. A person is considered vulnerable if they are in a weakened position that makes them more susceptible to manipulation. Vulnerability does not require a complete loss of legal capacity. It may result from advanced age, illness, cognitive impairment, emotional distress, or a growing dependence on others.

In California, adults aged 65 or older are considered part of a legally protected class under *Welfare and Institutions Code § 15610.27*. While age alone does not prove vulnerability, it becomes highly relevant when combined with other factors such as social isolation, medical decline, or reliance on a single individual for care or decision-making.

Proving vulnerability often involves demonstrating a pattern of behaviors or conditions rather than relying on isolated symptoms. Relevant factors may include recent hospitalizations, treatment for confusion or memory loss, or evaluations for conditions like depression or anxiety. Even without a formal diagnosis, circumstantial indicators, such as forgetting key information, frequent confusion, or reliance on one person for communication, can help establish a compelling case of vulnerability.

The following checklist highlights some of the signs of vulnerability commonly seen in probate cases. While not exhaustive, it provides a starting point for gathering evidence and identifying patterns that may support your claim (see Figure 9.1, *Checklist: Signs of Vulnerability*).

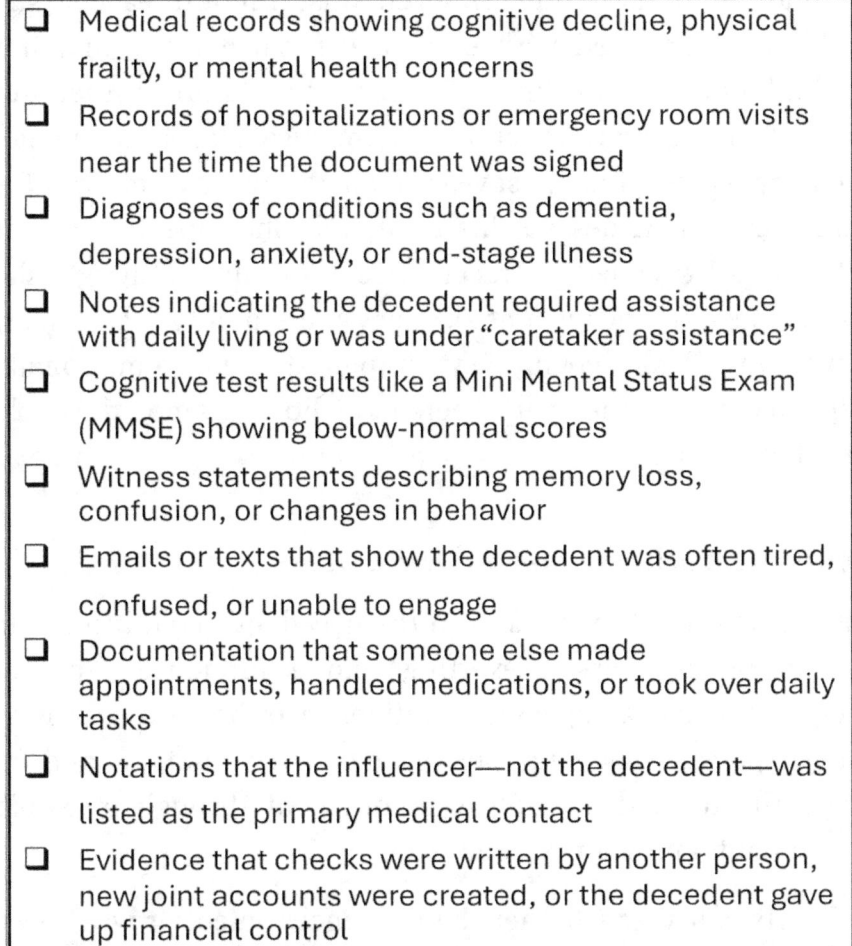

- ☐ Medical records showing cognitive decline, physical frailty, or mental health concerns
- ☐ Records of hospitalizations or emergency room visits near the time the document was signed
- ☐ Diagnoses of conditions such as dementia, depression, anxiety, or end-stage illness
- ☐ Notes indicating the decedent required assistance with daily living or was under "caretaker assistance"
- ☐ Cognitive test results like a Mini Mental Status Exam (MMSE) showing below-normal scores
- ☐ Witness statements describing memory loss, confusion, or changes in behavior
- ☐ Emails or texts that show the decedent was often tired, confused, or unable to engage
- ☐ Documentation that someone else made appointments, handled medications, or took over daily tasks
- ☐ Notations that the influencer—not the decedent—was listed as the primary medical contact
- ☐ Evidence that checks were written by another person, new joint accounts were created, or the decedent gave up financial control

Figure 9.1. Checklist: Signs of Vulnerability
This checklist helps identify signs of vulnerability that may support a claim of undue influence. It includes medical records, witness

statements, and evidence of dependency, highlighting factors that indicate the decedent's susceptibility to influence.

> **Our Experience**
>
> My mother was 81 when she signed the living trust that disinherited all six of her children. Just a month earlier, she had been diagnosed with end-stage renal disease, and her health had rapidly declined. The respondent, our brother and her full-time caregiver, reported to medical staff that she had memory issues for the past year and perseverative behavior for three years. I witnessed this firsthand. She repeated herself often and struggled to recall recent events. Although she wasn't legally incapacitated, her vulnerability was clear: physically frail, cognitively impaired, and emotionally dependent on the very person who became the sole beneficiary.

Apparent Authority of the Influencer

This factor shifts the focus from the decedent's condition to the position of the person exerting undue influence. Apparent authority means having control, influence, or perceived decision-making power that one person has over another and not necessarily through formal legal roles, but through proximity, involvement, and control of access.

Courts consider whether the influencer acted, or was viewed by others, as a trusted figure. This can include handling the decedent's daily needs, transportation, financial oversight, or health-related decisions (see Figure 9.2, *Checklist: Signs of*

Apparent Authority). Even if the influencer did not hold a formal role, their consistent involvement in the decedent's life can create an impression of authority.

> ❑ Records showing the influencer accompanied the decedent to medical or legal appointments
> ❑ Proof that the influencer made financial, legal, or housing decisions on the decedent's behalf
> ❑ Medical notes or legal documents listing the influencer as the decision-maker or main point of contact
> ❑ Texts or emails where the influencer speaks *for* the decedent ("She said...," "We decided...")
> ❑ Paperwork showing the influencer helped draft or coordinate legal or financial documents
> ❑ Bank statements showing the influencer managing funds or accessing accounts
> ❑ Evidence the influencer moved the decedent to a new residence or arranged care services
> ❑ Documentation of shared property transactions or payments between the decedent and influencer

Figure 9.2. Checklist: Signs of Apparent Authority
This checklist provides examples of situations where an individual had significant involvement in the decedent's life, such as managing finances, overseeing care, or making legal decisions. Such involvement may indicate influence or control, raising questions about undue influence.

> **Our Experience**
>
> Our brother gradually positioned himself as the central figure in our mother's life. He handled her medical appointments, managed her finances, and controlled who could visit or communicate with her. He moved her into his home and then into senior housing, often without discussing it with the family. Doctors and bank staff treated him as the primary decision-maker, reinforcing his apparent authority.
>
> Reflecting back, we didn't see the red flags at first. We only noticed that communication with our mother became increasingly strained. Texts from her would shift dramatically from asking for help to insisting we speak only with him. It wasn't clear to us at the time just how much control he had assumed or how isolated she had become.

Where the Two Factors Overlap

While these two factors are distinct, one describing the condition of the decedent, the other describing the position of the influencer, they often reinforce each other. A vulnerable person who is heavily dependent on a single caregiver may find it difficult to resist that person's suggestions. Likewise, someone who controls access to a vulnerable person can create an environment where manipulation thrives.

It's acceptable to reference the same facts in both sections of your petition, as long as the focus remains clear. One section should emphasize the *decedent's vulnerability*, while the other should highlight the *influencer's control*. This approach keeps the argument logically organized while acknowledging the interplay between these two factors.

Actions and tactics used

This factor focuses on the methods the influencer used to pressure, manipulate, or isolate the decedent. These tactics aren't always obvious. They're often psychological or emotional, such as stirring up fear, guilt, or confusion. The influencer may convince the decedent that others are untrustworthy or withhold important information. Methods like isolation, secrecy, and emotional manipulation can be just as powerful as direct threats. Figure 9.3 provides a checklist to better understand the types of tactics that may indicate undue influence (see Figure 9.3, *Checklist: Signs of Actions and Tactics Used*).

- ☐ Texts or voicemails where the influencer isolates the decedent ("She doesn't want to see you")
- ☐ Sudden changes in the decedent's tone or attitude toward loved ones—especially if repeating the influencer's language
- ☐ Emails or statements suggesting fear, guilt, or distrust planted by the influencer
- ☐ Timeline evidence showing secrecy (e.g., trust documents executed without notice to family)
- ☐ Documentation of the decedent's belongings being discarded, sold, or relocated without family input
- ☐ Contradictory messages—one day asking for help, the next insisting "talk to my lawyer"
- ☐ Testimony from relatives about emotional manipulation or mood swings
- ☐ Records showing limited or filtered access to the decedent

Figure 9.3. Checklist: Signs of Actions and Tactics Used

This checklist identifies behaviors that may indicate secrecy, emotional manipulation, or undue pressure. While these actions may not always leave a direct paper trail, recognizing patterns can help establish that the decedent's decisions did not reflect their true intentions.

> **Our Experience**
>
> Our brother repeatedly told our mother that we were jealous of him, framing himself as the only one she could trust. Eventually, his words became hers, and during her perseverative episodes, she would repeat his praises almost verbatim.
>
> His actions were shrouded in secrecy. He sold her house without telling us. We only learned it had been on the market after the sale was complete. He also arranged for the creation of the living trust without informing us. When confronted, he claimed that our mother had disinherited us because we were estranged despite clear evidence to the contrary, like family photos taken shortly before and after the trust was signed.
>
> One text message from her read, *"I just want to die. Instead of being helpful, he's abusive."* A few days later, her tone completely shifted, telling us to stop interfering. It was as if her thoughts were no longer entirely her own.

Inequity of the Result

An outcome that disproportionately benefits one person—especially at the expense of long-standing heirs or relationships—can indicate undue influence. Sudden, unexplained changes to an estate plan that differ from the decedent's past intentions may raise concerns. Such changes **often alter** the distribution of assets in a way that favors one person over others who were previously included. To help identify signs of inequity, see Figure 9.4, *Checklist: Signs of Inequity of the Result*.

- ☐ Final trust or will documents that dramatically differ from prior versions
- ☐ The influencer named as both sole beneficiary and trustee (or other dual-benefit roles)
- ☐ The decedent's own writings or statements contradicting the final distribution (texts, emails, letters)
- ☐ Disinheritance of long-standing heirs with no explanation or warning. Omission of people who were closely involved in the decedent's life
- ☐ Inclusion of unusual or outdated information (e.g., listing a child who passed away decades earlier)
- ☐ Copies of earlier trusts or estate plans showing a very different distribution pattern
- ☐ Witness statements that the decedent previously intended to divide assets more equally

Figure 9.4. Checklist: Signs of Inequity of the Result
This checklist outlines outcomes that may appear unexpected, unbalanced, or inconsistent with the decedent's previous intentions. While individuals have the right to choose how they distribute their assets, sudden or dramatic changes, especially without explanation, may warrant closer examination.

> **Our Experience**
>
> In our case, both the original trust and its amendment disinherited all the children, leaving everything to our brother. One detail immediately stood out: I was named as successor trustee, despite being disinherited. This made no sense. Why would she entrust me with fiduciary responsibility but leave me nothing? The inconsistency suggested that something was off.
>
> Another odd detail was that the amendment disinherited a sibling who had died in 1957. This mistake indicated a lack of awareness or understanding when the document was signed. It was as if the decedent didn't fully comprehend the content or implications of the amendment.

Clarity Comes with Persistence

It took nearly three years to piece together the full story. When I first filed our petition, I didn't have the right legal language or all the evidence. I just knew something wasn't right. Over time, through persistent research and documentation, I began to see the pattern of manipulation and control.

At first, it felt overwhelming. The story wasn't clear, the evidence was scattered, and the emotional toll was heavy. But bit by bit, I organized what I had, including medical records, text messages, family photos, and learned how to present it legally. The process was hard, but I kept going because I believed in the truth.

That's how you build a case, not with certainty, but with persistence. You don't need the perfect story to begin. You just need to start.

Undue influence is challenging to prove because it happens quietly and subtly. You may feel like you're fighting an uphill battle, but persistence and a clear, organized presentation of the facts can make a difference. Stay focused on gathering evidence, documenting patterns, and telling the story as accurately as possible. When the legal pieces come together, your case becomes more than just a feeling. It becomes a compelling legal argument.

> **Pro Tip:** When gathering evidence for undue influence, focus on patterns rather than isolated incidents. A single moment of confusion might not prove your case, but a documented history of manipulation strengthens your argument.

Cause of Action III: Financial Elder Abuse

Financial elder abuse happens when someone uses manipulation, deception, coercion, Financial elder abuse occurs when someone manipulates, deceives, coerces, or exerts undue influence to gain control over the financial assets of a person aged 65 or older. Under California law (*Welfare and Institutions Code § 15610.30*), this doesn't just include outright theft or fraud. It also covers situations where someone assists in or benefits from wrongfully taking or keeping an elder's property, even when it appears to be "help" on the surface.

This kind of abuse rarely starts with force. Instead, it often begins with trust. A caregiver or family member may gradually take over financial tasks, handling bills, accessing accounts, or transferring property, while the elder's health and independence quietly decline.

Our Experience: Uncovering Financial Elder Abuse

In our case, we eventually learned that when our mother sold her primary residence in 2013, where she had lived for 50 years, she never filed taxes on the sale. Her attorney later stated that, with interest and penalties, she owed approximately $700,000 in unpaid capital gains tax. But the more alarming issue was that the proceeds from the $635,000 sale were never properly accounted for. At the time of the sale, she was already 80 years old and showing noticeable cognitive decline. Yet two years later, she had been moved into a senior facility with no explanation of how those substantial funds were used.

We discovered that some of the money used for the respondent's business expenses, including the purchase of equipment, had come from our mother. In his responses to our Requests for Admissions (RFAs), he admitted that she had paid for the equipment, but he never clarified where that money came from. Later, he claimed that the trust was responsible for the tax debt but couldn't explain what had happened to the money from the house sale. To us, it appeared she had been used to finance his needs masked as assistance.

One particularly confusing claim was that the debt was part of the trust, but the proceeds from the sale were not. It didn't add

> up. How could the trust inherit the liability but not the funds? This inconsistency highlighted the financial manipulation we suspected all along.

Warning Signs of Financial Elder Abuse

Financial elder abuse can manifest in various ways. Here are some signs that may indicate a problem:

- Large or unexplained transfers of money
- Sudden changes in property titles or beneficiary designations
- Missing bank records or refusal to share financial information
- An elderly person unexpectedly funding another person's business, lifestyle, or debts
- Vague explanations like "she wanted it that way," without documentation or clarity
- A trust or will that contradicts the elder's previously stated intentions or values

Taking Legal Action

In probate court, petitions to recover assets can be filed under Probate Code § 850. If elder abuse is proven, *Probate Code § 259* may be used to disqualify the abuser from inheriting under the trust or will. However, none of this can happen unless the issue is raised and investigated.

Even if you don't have all the answers initially, identifying signs of financial abuse can justify a deeper investigation.

Sometimes, the cumulative effect of seemingly small irregularities can reveal a pattern of financial exploitation.

Cause of Action IV: Breach of Fiduciary Duty

When someone is appointed as a trustee, executor, or agent under a power of attorney, they are legally bound by a **fiduciary duty**. This means they must act in the best interests of the estate and its beneficiaries and not for their own personal gain. In California, these duties are outlined in *California Probate Code §§ 16000–16015*, which defines fiduciary responsibilities such as loyalty, impartiality, and care.

Key Fiduciary Duties

A **fiduciary** is a person or entity legally obligated to act in the best interest of another party. Their primary obligation is to act with loyalty and impartiality, meaning they must prioritize the interests of all beneficiaries equally. Favoritism is prohibitive. For example, if a trustee has siblings who are co-beneficiaries, they cannot allocate more assets to themselves or make decisions that disproportionately benefit one person over another.

Fiduciaries are also required to maintain transparency by keeping beneficiaries reasonably informed about the trust and its administration. This includes providing annual accountings that clearly show:

- The financial status of the trust at the start and end of the year
- Income earned, expenses paid, and how assets were managed.

- Supporting documentation, such as receipts, bank statements, and explanations for significant transactions

If the trust pays for something, the fiduciary must be able to justify why the expense was necessary and how it aligns with the trust's purpose.

Another critical duty is to avoid conflicts of interest and self-dealing. A fiduciary must not use estate assets for personal benefit. For instance, if the fiduciary uses trust funds to buy equipment for their own business, that could be seen as *self-dealing*—especially if there is no documentation showing that the purchase directly benefited the estate.

Fiduciaries must also exercise care in financial management. Under *Probate Code § 16047*, trustees must act as prudent investors, meaning they should make financial decisions that preserve the estate's value while also seeking reasonable growth. This could involve placing liquid assets in interest-bearing accounts rather than letting them sit idle. For example, if the estate includes significant cash holdings, the trustee should invest them prudently rather than leaving them in a non-interest-bearing checking account.

Failing to uphold these duties can constitute a breach of fiduciary duty, which is a legal cause of action in probate court. If a fiduciary fails to provide proper accountings, mismanages assets, or uses funds for personal purposes without justification, beneficiaries can file a petition to remove the trustee and recover lost assets.

Our Experience

In our case, the respondent became trustee in 2015, yet he failed to provide any financial accounting for more than seven years. When he finally submitted one, it was incomplete, missing key documentation, transaction histories, and supporting receipts. An annual accounting should clearly state what the trust held at the start of the year, what income came in, what was paid out (and why), and what remained at year's end. Instead, we received a vague summary with gaps and missing records.

One of the most troubling issues was that, despite the trust's Schedule A listing assets like bank accounts, stocks, IRAs, a limited partnership, and vacant land, there was no clear indication of what happened to these items. To this day, most of those assets remain unaccounted for.

We also discovered that the respondent had been referring to one property as "his house" for years, even though it had been part of the trust. After our mother passed away in 2022, he transferred title into his own name just three months later, which triggered a property tax reassessment that doubled the taxes, which then became delinquent. This action not only raised legal concerns but also financially damaged the estate.

In his written responses to our discovery requests, the respondent admitted that our mother had purchased much of the equipment used in his business. While that alone may not definitively prove wrongdoing, it added to a pattern of using trust assets as personal property. At no point did he notify us, seek court approval, or explain how trust funds were spent.

> Looking back, I realized that persistence and a methodical approach were my best allies. I didn't need a perfect case from the start. I just needed a willingness to dig deeper and stay focused on the truth.

Key Fiduciary Duties

When managing a trust, a fiduciary is legally obligated to fulfill several key duties to ensure the proper administration and protection of the estate's assets. These duties are essential to maintaining trust and fairness among all beneficiaries.

Loyalty and Impartiality

The fiduciary must act solely in the interests of all beneficiaries, without favoritism. This duty requires treating co-beneficiaries fairly, regardless of personal relationships. Any action that prioritizes one beneficiary over another, without legal justification, may be deemed a breach of fiduciary duty.

Transparency, Communication, and Record Keeping

Beneficiaries have the right to be kept informed about the trust's administration. This duty requires fiduciaries to provide *annual accountings* that detail the estate's financial status at the beginning and end of the year. These accountings must include:

- Income received
- Expenses paid
- Changes in assets
- Supporting documents, such as bank statements, receipts, invoices, contracts, and clear explanations for significant transactions (e.g., property sales or large withdrawals)

According to *Probate Code § 16060* and *§ 16062*, fiduciaries must ensure that these records are comprehensive and accurate. Failing to maintain or provide these records may result in legal consequences and could be considered a breach of fiduciary duty.

A fiduciary must also maintain detailed records of all financial transactions made on behalf of the estate. This practice ensures that every financial decision is properly documented and traceable, protecting the estate and beneficiaries from potential mismanagement.

Additional Fiduciary Duties

Avoidance of Self-Dealing

Fiduciaries must not use trust assets for personal gain or make decisions that benefit themselves at the expense of the estate. Any action that appears to serve the fiduciary's interests over those of the beneficiaries could be considered **self-dealing**, a clear breach of duty (*Probate Code § 16004*).

Prudent Investment

Trustees are expected to preserve and grow trust assets. This includes investing wisely, such as placing liquid assets in interest-bearing accounts rather than allowing them to sit idle. The **Prudent Investor Rule** (Probate Code § 16047) requires fiduciaries to balance risk and reward while maintaining the estate's financial stability.

Preservation of Assets

Fiduciaries should actively manage the estate to ensure that assets are protected and maintained. This includes paying taxes on time, securing properties, and making financial decisions that prevent loss or devaluation.

If a fiduciary fails to uphold these duties, such as by neglecting to file taxes, using funds for personal business, or not providing accountings, they may be held accountable in probate court. Beneficiaries can file a petition to remove the trustee, recover lost assets, or seek damages for financial harm caused by mismanagement.

Consequences of Breaching Fiduciary Duty

If a fiduciary fails to uphold these duties, such as by neglecting to file taxes, using funds for personal business, or not providing accountings. They may be held accountable in probate court. Beneficiaries can file a petition to remove the trustee, recover lost assets, or seek damages for financial harm caused by mismanagement.

Other Potential Grounds

In addition to common causes of action like undue influence or financial elder abuse, there are other legal grounds that may justify contesting a trust or will. These claims are less frequently used in probate petitions, not because they are less valid, but because they often require a higher burden of proof. To succeed, they usually depend on strong supporting evidence such as witness declarations, handwriting analysis, or expert testimony.

Fraud

Fraud occurs when the decedent was intentionally deceived, such as being lied to about the contents of a document or being misled about what they were signing. For example, someone might claim that a document was "just a form" or "just temporary," when in fact it changed the entire estate plan. To prove fraud, it's crucial to show that the decedent relied on false information when making decisions about their estate.

Duress

Duress involves situations where the decedent was coerced or threatened into signing a trust or amendment against their will. This could include fear, intimidation, or pressure from someone in a position of control or dependency. Evidence may include witness testimony, written threats, or behavioral changes observed during the time the document was executed.

Forgery

Forgery means the decedent's signature was falsified or that the document was altered after they signed it. Proving forgery can be challenging, as it often relies on expert handwriting analysis or forensic evidence. Sometimes, discrepancies in signature style, ink types, or paper age may also support this claim.

Mistake

Mistake may apply if the decedent misunderstood what they were signing, perhaps due to confusion, poor communication, or misrepresentation of the document's purpose. For example, the decedent might have believed they were signing a power of attorney form when it was actually a trust amendment. Demonstrating mistake often involves showing that the decedent was misled or lacked clarity about the document's nature.

The Challenge and the Opportunity

If you believe any of these grounds may apply, it's important to know that the court will expect highly specific evidence. While these claims can be harder to prove, they can also be powerful tools—especially when something about the situation feels off but doesn't clearly fall under more common categories. In some instances, these lesser-used legal theories can be the key to uncovering and correcting serious wrongdoing.

When exploring these grounds, persistence is essential. Even when the evidence is difficult to gather, staying vigilant and methodical in your investigation can make the difference. Sometimes, it's not about having the perfect case from the start but about identifying overlooked facts that may ultimately support your claim.

Conclusion

Challenging a trust or will is a complex legal process that requires more than just a sense of injustice. It demands a well-structured argument grounded in law and supported by evidence. By understanding the legal grounds for contesting a trust or will, such as lack of capacity, undue influence, financial elder abuse, and breach of fiduciary duty, you equip yourself with the tools to build a compelling case.

It's important to remember that these causes of action are not merely labels. They are legal frameworks that guide how your story is presented in court. Each claim requires specific evidence, legal reasoning, and a clear connection between the facts and the law. Even lesser-used grounds, like fraud or mistake, can be critical when the more common claims don't quite fit.

Contesting a trust or will is not just about presenting facts. It's about demonstrating how those facts add up to a legal violation. Stay focused on gathering strong evidence, organizing your story clearly, and pushing forward even when the path is uncertain. Your persistence can make the difference between a dismissed case and a successful challenge.

To summarize the essential concepts covered in this chapter and help you build a legally sound petition for contesting a trust or will, Figure 9.5 highlights the key takeaways from Chapter 9 (see Figure 9.5, *Key Takeaways – Legal Grounds*). Use it as a practical reference when preparing your case.

1. Contesting a trust or will requires specific legal grounds (causes of action), not just a sense of unfairness.
2. The most common causes include lack of capacity, undue influence, financial elder abuse, and breach of fiduciary duty. Each must demonstrate that a legal rule was violated.
3. Lack of capacity means the decedent may not have understood what they were signing. Evidence may include medical records, witness statements, or expert evaluations.
4. Undue influence involves excessive pressure on a vulnerable person, often proven through patterns of control, manipulation, or isolation.
5. Financial elder abuse is the wrongful control of an elder's assets through manipulation or deception. Look for signs like sudden financial changes or misuse of funds.
6. Breach of fiduciary duty occurs when a trustee acts for personal gain rather than the beneficiaries' interests, often involving self-dealing or poor asset management.
7. Other grounds like fraud, duress, forgery, or mistake require strong, specific evidence.
8. Focus on *building patterns of evidence* rather than finding one "perfect" piece. Persistence may make the difference.

Figure 9.5. Key Takeaways – Legal Grounds
Summarizes the most common legal grounds—lack of capacity, undue influence, elder abuse, and breach of fiduciary duty—and emphasizes the need for strong evidence and persistence.

CHAPTER 10

Procedural Requirements

Introduction

Meeting the court's procedural requirements is just as important as presenting strong legal arguments. Courts sometimes enforce strict formatting, structural, and filing standards, even for self-represented (pro per) litigants, and failing to comply can result in delays or outright rejection of your petition. A well-organized title page not only meets legal requirements but also ensures that your petition is processed efficiently. This chapter covers formatting and structural rules, required forms and attachments, and key technical aspects of how petitions must be submitted whether in person, by mail, or electronically.

> **Note:** The formatting guidelines in this chapter are based on the California Rules of Court and are written with Los Angeles County in mind. These practices are widely accepted throughout the state, but it is important to remember that each courthouse may have its own local rules or preferences. If you are filing in a different county-or in another state entirely-be sure to check with your local probate court. Many courts publish local rules on their website or provide information by phone. Following your court's specific formatting requirements is essential to having your documents accepted.

General Formatting and Structural Requirements

Although formatting errors alone may not result in rejection, adhering to standard guidelines significantly improves the clarity and professionalism of your petition. Most California probate courts require documents to be formatted on pleading paper—pages with 28 numbered lines and specific margin widths (*California Rules of Court, Rule 2.111*). Even if your local court allows other formats, using pleading paper is generally the safest option.

Standard margin guidelines include at least one inch on the top and bottom, at least 0.5 inch on the right side, and at least one inch on the left side, in accordance with *California Rules of Court, Rule 2.107*. A slightly wider left margin, such as 1.25 inches, is optional and may be used to accommodate binding (see Figure 10.1, *Sample 28-Line Pleading Paper*).

Figure 10.1. Sample 28-Line Pleading Paper
Blank pleading page formatted according to California Rule of Court 2.111. Most California probate courts require this format to ensure professional and consistent presentation

Most courts also require petitions to be formatted in a legible font. The most commonly accepted fonts are 12-point Times New Roman or Courier, though some courts allow Arial (*California Rules of Court, Rule 2.105*). The lines on each page must be one-and-one-half spaced or double-spaced and numbered consecutively, except for headings, footnotes, and certain elements of the title page. Headings are typically single-spaced and bolded or underlined for clarity (Do not use both bold and underline unless required by your local court). Footnotes remain single-spaced with one blank line between each footnote to improve readability.

Once the formatting is set, the first page of the petition must follow a structured layout known as the Title Page. This page provides essential case details, including the petitioner's information, court jurisdiction, case number, and the petition title (*California Rules of Court, Rule 2.111(1)*). Properly formatting the title page ensures that the court can efficiently process the petition, and that all necessary information is clearly presented.

The Title Page

The title page must follow a specific format to ensure proper filing (*California Rules of Court, Rules 2.100–2.119*). At the top left, list the petitioner's full name in all capital letters, followed by "In Pro Per" to indicate self-representation. Below the name, provide the petitioner's mailing address, phone number, and email address in single-spaced format.

Two lines below the petitioner's information, the name of the court should be centered and written in all caps as: "SUPERIOR

COURT OF THE STATE OF CALIFORNIA." Directly below, also centered, list the county name in all capital letters. For example, if filing in Los Angeles County, write "COUNTY OF LOS ANGELES."

Two spaces below the county name, there must be a boxed section divided into two columns. The left side of the box contains three sections. At the top of the left column, write the title of the trust or contested document in all caps, such as "IN RE: THE JANE DOE TRUST DATED JANUARY 20, 2025" or "IN THE MATTER OF DOE ESTATE." Below the horizontal line, list the petitioner's name, labeled as "[YOUR NAME(S)], Petitioner(s)." Directly below, list the respondent's name, labeled as "[Opposing Party's Name], Respondent."

Note: Understanding DOES 1–10 in Legal Filings

In some probate cases, you may not know the names of all involved parties at the time of filing. To address this, California law allows you to list a placeholder names, commonly referred to as "DOES 1-10" (*California Code of Civil Procedure § 474*). This allows the petitioner to amend the petition later if additional parties are identified. If there are suspected individuals who played a role in undue influence or mismanagement, but their identities are currently unknown, naming DOES 1–10 ensures they can be added later without refiling the entire case. In the Background section of your petition, you should clarify that their real names will be substituted when known. For example:

"Petitioner names DOES 1–10 as fictitious respondents whose true names and capacities are unknown at this time. Petitioner will amend this Petition to allege their true names and capacities when they are ascertained."

The right side of the title page box includes six sections. At the top, label the first section "Case #:" and leave it blank. This is where the court will fill in the case number. Directly below that, write the title of the petition in all capital letters and bold. For example:

"PETITION TO INVALIDATE A LIVING TRUST BASED ON UNDUE INFLUENCE AND LACK OF CAPACITY."

Below the petition title, list the applicable Probate Code sections in brackets, such as "[Probate Code §§ 850, 17200, 16061.7]." (These are just examples. Be sure to include only the specific code sections that apply to your petition.)

The remaining sections are labeled "DATE:," "TIME:," "LOCATION:," and "JUDGE." Each of these should also be left blank (see Figure 10.2, *Sample Title Page with Annotations*). The court will complete these details upon filing.

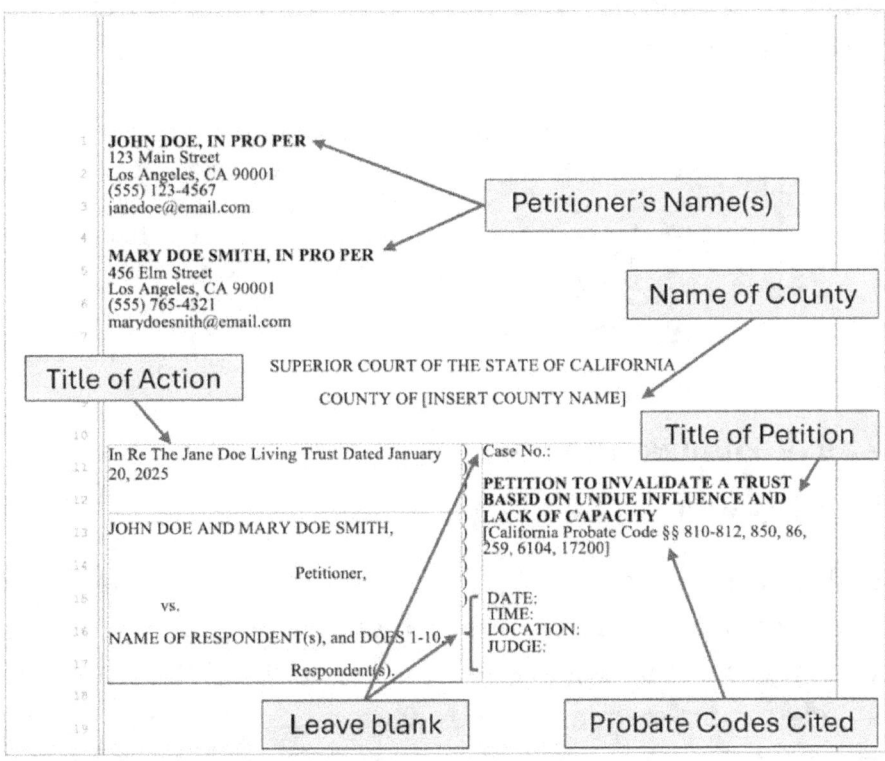

Figure 10.2. Sample Title Page with Annotations
Properly formatted title page showing required elements, including petitioner information, court details, and a caption box with space for the case number and hearing information. Follows California Rules of Court 2.100–2.119.

It is essential to follow the correct formatting for spacing, bolding, and capitalization to ensure that the document is properly structured.

Download the Petition Template

Before you continue through the step-by-step breakdown below, I recommend downloading the Petition Template. This template follows the structure you'll be learning in the remainder of this chapter, with standard headings, fill-in-the-blank prompts, and procedural guidance.

> **Organize Your Petition.** Follow the **Petition Template** to assemble your petition. Download it at https://properprobate.guide/california-filing or scan  the QR code. It is designed to help you structure your full draft using standard court headings and stay procedurally on track.

Body of Your Petition

Headings and Subheadings

Legal petitions use a structured system of headings and subheadings to organize information, guide the reader, and clearly present legal arguments. This hierarchical structure helps the judge, court staff, and opposing parties understand the flow of your petition and identify key points. Headings also make your document easier to navigate and more professional in appearance.

There are four common levels of headings used in California probate petitions. Each level reflects a different level of detail, and each one follows a specific formatting style. Regardless of how many levels you use, always begin with the first-level heading and move downward only when needed. Headings should be used consistently and clearly throughout your document.

First-level headings identify the major sections of your petition. These use Roman numerals (I., II., III.), and should be bold, all capital letters, and centered. They begin on their own line and signal a new section in the document. In this guide, we begin with:

I. INTRODUCTION

This heading sets the stage for your petition. In your introduction, you can briefly explain what you are asking the court to do and why. After the introduction, most petitions proceed to a section titled **II. FACTUAL BACKGROUND**, which outlines the facts that support your request.

Second-level subheadings appear within a first-level section and divide it into distinct claims or categories. These use capital letters (A., B., C.), are bold and in all caps, and may be either centered or aligned to the left. Each subheading begins on its own line. For example:

A. LACK OF CAPACITY

Third-level subheadings fall under a second-level subheading and are used to introduce the elements of a legal test, such as the four factors of undue influence. These use lowercase Roman numerals (i., ii., iii.) and are written in *sentence case*, which means only the first word is capitalized unless it is a proper noun. The subheading appears on the *same line* as the paragraph that follows. I choose not to italicize these headings, as this is not common in legal pleadings. For example:

1. **Vulnerability of the victim** – The decedent was elderly and diagnosed with dementia at the time the trust amendment was signed. Evidence of her cognitive decline includes the following:

Fourth-level list items are used to present specific facts or examples that support the third-level paragraph above. These are not headings. They use lowercase letters (a., b., c.) and are written in sentence case. Each list item appears on its own line and is indented slightly from the left margin to visually separate it from the paragraph. For example:

    a. Decedent was diagnosed with dementia in 2018.
    b. She relied on the respondent for transportation and medication.
    c. Medical records confirm progressive cognitive decline.

This multi-level structure is not required by court rule, but it reflects how attorneys write and how judges process legal arguments. Using it in your petition improves clarity, professionalism, and readability.

For a visual example of this heading system, see Figure 10.3, *Sample Heading Structure for a Probate Petition*.

> **II. FACTUAL BACKGROUND**
>
> **A. LACK OF CAPACITY**
>
> **B. UNDUE INFLUENCE**
>
>   i. Vulnerability of the victim – The decedent was elderly...
>
>   a. She was diagnosed in 2018.
>
>   b. She relied on the respondent...
>
>   c. Records confirm memory loss.

Figure 10.3. Sample Heading Structure for a Petition
A four-level heading system commonly used in California probate petitions. The structure includes first-level headings (Roman numerals, bold, all caps, centered) for major sections, followed by second-level subheadings (capital letters, bold, all caps). Third-level subheadings (lowercase Roman numerals, sentence case), followed by fourth-level (lowercase letters, sentence case).

For a formatting summary that outlines the structure and purpose of each heading level, see Table 10.1, *Legal Heading Levels and Formatting Guide.*

Table 10.1. Legal Heading Levels and Formatting Guide

Level	Format
1	**Centered, bold, ALL CAPS, Roman numerals.** Starts a new section on its own line
2	**Centered or flush-left, bold, ALL CAPS, capital letters (A., B., C.).** Starts a new subsection on its own line
3	**Flush-left, sentence case, lowercase Roman numerals (i., ii., iii.).** Appears on the same line as the paragraph text. Used to introduce elements of a legal test or factor
4	**Indented, sentence case, lowercase letters (a., b., c.).** Used for listing specific examples or evidence. Not a heading. Appears as part of a paragraph or list

Note. A quick-reference guide to the four levels of headings commonly used in California probate petitions. It includes the formatting style for each level, such as capitalization, alignment, and numbering, and explains where each heading appears in relation to the text.

Paragraph Numbering and Indentation

In court pleadings, each paragraph must be numbered and begin on a new line. According to *California Rules of Court, Rule 2.111(3)*, paragraph numbers must continue in sequence throughout the entire document and should not restart under new headings or subheadings.

Although the rules do not require indentation, most professionally prepared petitions use a *first-line indent*, where both the paragraph number and the first sentence are offset slightly from the left margin (see Figure 10.4, *Sample Paragraph Numbering and Indentation*). This format improves readability, mirrors how attorneys write, and aligns with the expectations of judges and court staff. Each paragraph should stand alone as a clear and complete unit of thought, properly numbered and visually distinct from those around it.

> **II. FACTUAL BACKGROUND**
>
> 1. Petitioner is the daughter of the decedent and brings this action to challenge the validity of the trust amendment executed on March 3, 2021. The decedent was diagnosed with moderate dementia in 2019. Two years prior to her diagnosis, she began exhibiting signs of cognitive decline and required increasing assistance with daily tasks during the final two years of her life.
>
> 2. The decedent was diagnosed with moderate dementia in 2019 and required increasing assistance with daily tasks during the final two years of life.
>
> 3. Petitioner alleges that the respondent exerted undue influence over the decedent at a time when she lacked sufficient mental capacity to understand or resist changes to her estate plan.

Figure 10.4. Sample Paragraph Numbering and Indentation
Formatting paragraphs within a probate petition with each paragraph starting on a new line, numbered sequentially, and a slight first-line indent for improved readability.

Footer Formatting

At the bottom of each page, include a footer that restates the full title of your petition in *all capital letters*, centered, and followed by the *page number* (see Figure 10.5, *Sample Footer with Title and Page Number*). The font should be no smaller than 10-point to ensure readability. This formatting helps preserve the integrity of your document—especially if pages become separated during scanning, filing, or review. A properly formatted footer also reinforces the professional appearance of your petition and makes it easier for the court to keep track of multiple filings.

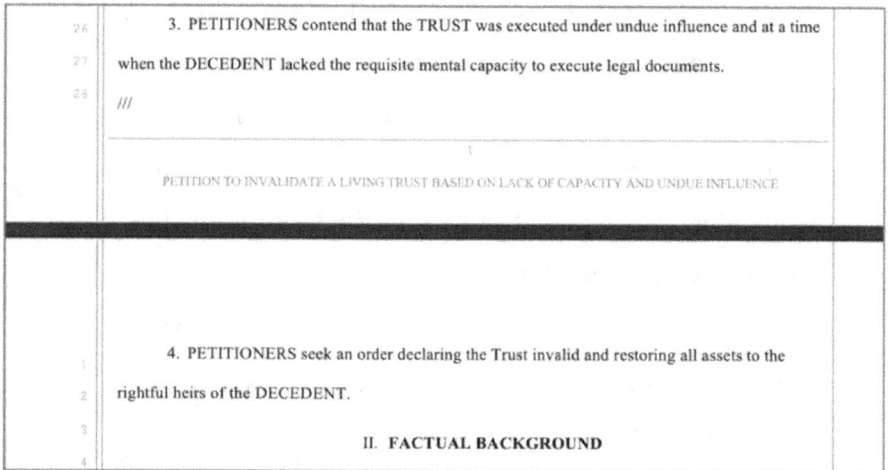

Figure 10.5. Sample Footer with Title and Page Number
Example of a footer format for a petition. The footer displays the full title in all capital letters, centered at the bottom, followed by the page number. This format ensures clear labeling, proper order, and easy identification, even if pages become separated. The font should be at least 10-point for readability.

What to Include with Your Petition: Required Documents

Supporting Documents

When filing a petition to invalidate a will or trust, the petition itself serves as the foundational document, outlining the legal arguments, supporting facts, and requested relief. However, probate courts expect petitioners to include enough supporting documentation to demonstrate that their claims have merit (*California Probate Code § 8252*). Failing to provide key documents can result in delays, additional court hearings, or outright rejection of the petition (*California Rules of Court, Rule 7.104*). These same principles apply to other common probate petitions, such as those involving fraud, breach of fiduciary duty, or failure to provide an accounting.

While the court does not require you to submit your entire body of evidence at the time of filing, it is important to attach certain core documents that support your case—especially if they are already in your possession. These typically include a *copy of the trust or will being contested,* any *prior versions* or *amendments* that show significant changes, and, if available, *sworn declarations* or *medical records* that support your legal claims. Including these upfront helps establish that your petition is based on more than speculation. If you are alleging lack of capacity, for example, attaching relevant medical records early on can be persuasive. If you are alleging undue influence, a declaration from someone who witnessed the decedent's vulnerability or the respondent's control may help support your position.

Additional documentation, such as witness statements, financial records, and correspondence, can often be submitted later during the *discovery phase* of your case. That stage, covered in a future volume of this guide, allows you to formally request evidence from the opposing party and supplement the record with more detailed proof. However, the stronger your petition is at the time of filing, the more seriously the court will take your claims from the start.

Supporting documents vary depending on the legal grounds for the petition. If the challenge involves undue influence, sworn declarations or affidavits from witnesses who observed the decedent's interactions with the alleged influencer may be crucial (*California Probate Code § 86*). If the challenge is based on lack of capacity, medical records must be submitted to demonstrate the decedent's cognitive state at the time the trust or will was executed (California Probate Code § 811). Financial disputes often require bank statements, tax returns, or asset valuations to prove mismanagement or improper transfers. Additionally, written witness statements from individuals with direct knowledge of the estate's administration or the trust's execution can serve as valuable evidence. These supporting documents need to be included as Exhibits in the petition (*California Rules of Court, Rule 3.1110(f)*).

For further guidance on gathering evidence, please see Chapter 5: Possible Evidence to Support Your Claim.

Exhibits

All supporting evidence must be referenced within the petition and attached as an exhibit at the end of the document (California

Rules of Court, Rule 3.1110(f)). Whenever you refer to a document that you are attaching as an exhibit, such as a trust, an amendment, or a medical record, you should clearly reference that document in the body of your petition and match it to the labeled exhibit at the end of the document (see Figure 10.6, *Sample Petition Referencing Exhibit A*)..

For example, in the opening section of a petition, your references might look like this:

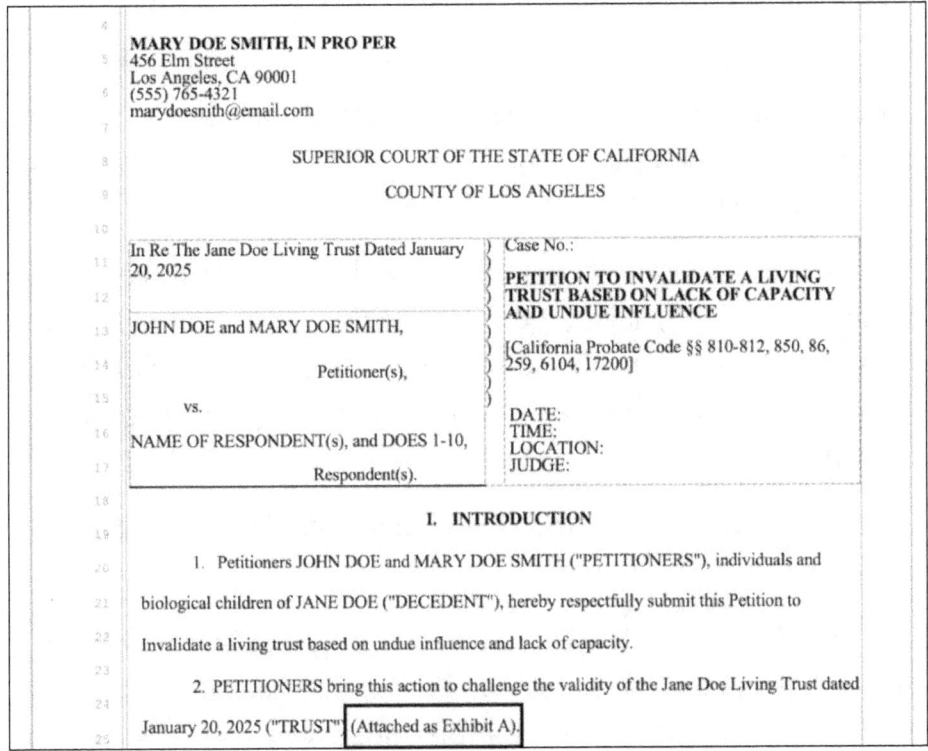

Figure 10.6. Sample Petition Referencing Exhibit A
Example of how to introduce a trust document within a petition. The phrase "attached as Exhibit A" appears in paragraph 2, indicating that the referenced document will be included at the end of the petition under the same label.

In paragraph 2, the petition clearly identifies the document being challenged and immediately links it to Exhibit A using the phrase (Attached as Exhibit A). This tells the court: (1) What the document is, (2) Why it's important to the petition, and (3) Where to find it at the end of the filing.

The language used here, such as "TRUST", placed in quotation marks and capitalized, signals to the court that this is a defined term that will be used throughout the petition. This makes your petition easier to read and more consistent.

Once a document is introduced with its full name and exhibit label, you can refer to it in a shorter form throughout the rest of the petition, such as simply the "TRUST" or "Exhibit A," depending on the context.

At the end of the petition, the actual document must appear under the matching label, Exhibit A, so the court can easily locate it. In Figure 10.7, *Sample Exhibit Cover Page for Attachments*, it shows how that exhibit should appear, including a clearly marked cover page that reads:

"EXHIBIT A – The Jane Doe Living Trust Dated January 20, 2025."

This *cover page* is not part of the original document. It's a simple title page you create and place in front of the trust. It tells the court exactly what the exhibit is and gives it a clear label. The trust document itself then follows this cover page as part of the exhibit.

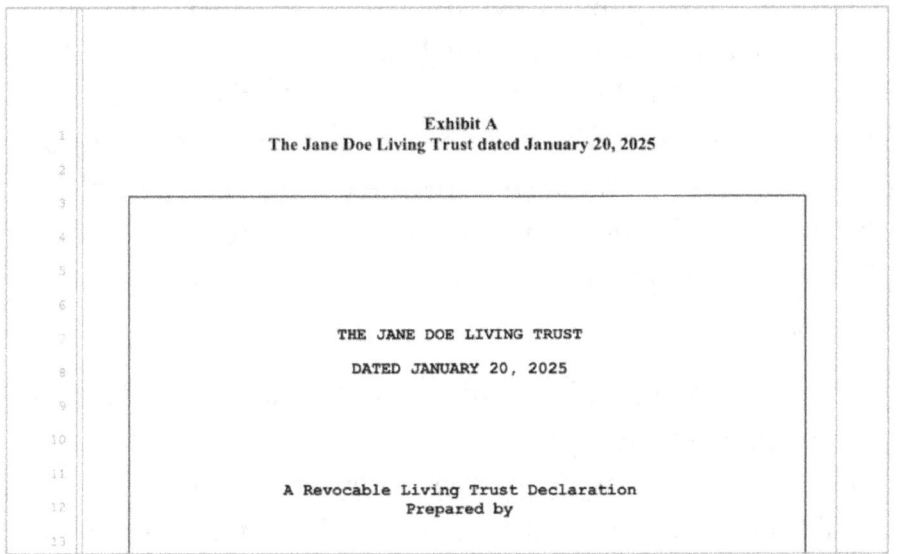

Figure 10.7. Sample Exhibit Cover Page for Attachments
Example of a properly formatted exhibit cover page labeled "EXHIBIT A – The Jane Doe Living Trust dated January 20, 2025." introducing the trust document referenced in the petition followed by the complete trust without any additional markings.

This consistent structure, which involves referencing the exhibit clearly in the petition and attaching it with a matching exhibit label, ensures that the court can cross-reference your arguments with the supporting evidence quickly and efficiently.

Courts prefer exhibits to be labeled in alphabetical order (Exhibit A, Exhibit B, etc.) and presented in a clearly organized format. If you are filing a paper copy, each exhibit should be separated by a physical tab. These tabs (typically plastic or paper) protrude slightly from the edge of the document to help the court quickly locate specific sections.

If you are filing electronically, exhibits should be *bookmarked*. This means adding hyperlinks within the PDF that allow the court to click and jump directly to the corresponding exhibit at the end of the document (*California Rules of Court, Rule 3.1110(f)(4)*). While not required, I also hyperlink each exhibit back to the location in the petition where it was originally referenced. This creates a two-way navigation system for the court's convenience.

Proper labeling and organization enhance accessibility and ensure the court can efficiently locate relevant information, ultimately strengthening the credibility of your petition. Well-organized exhibits not only improve clarity but also increase the persuasive impact of your claims.

How to Introduce and Refer to People in Your Petition

In legal petitions, especially in probate court, it is standard practice to introduce each person involved in the case using their full legal name in all capital letters, followed by a shortened label in parentheses. This label, such as "PETITIONERS," "RESPONDENT," or "DECEDENT", is used consistently throughout the rest of the petition to keep your writing clear and professional.

For example, you might write: JOHN DOE and MARY SMITH ("PETITIONERS"), biological children of JANE DOE ("DECEDENT"), bring this action against ROBERT TAYLOR. ("RESPONDENT"), successor trustee of THE JANE DOE LIVING TRUST DATED JANUARY 20, 2025 ("TRUST"). The use of all caps helps the court distinguish parties at a glance, and the label in parentheses allows you to reference each person or document easily throughout the rest of your petition. The use of consistent party labels throughout your petition improves clarity and professionalism (see Table 10.2, *Common Legal Role Labels in a Probate Petition*).

Table 10.2. Common Legal Role Labels in a Probate Petition

Title/Name	Legal Role and When to Use It
SETTLOR/TRUSTOR	Person who created the trust. Use when referring to actions while alive
DECEDENT	The person who has died. Used when referring to estate matters after death
TRUSTEE	Person who manages the trust. May be RESPONDENT in contested matters
RESPONDENT	Person the petition is filed against—often the trustee or beneficiary
DEFENDANT	Person being sued in civil court. Like RESPONDENT but used outside of probate
EXECUTOR	Person named in a will to carry out decedent's wishes and manage estate
ADMINISTRATOR	Court-appointed to manage the estate when there is no will (intestate succession)
PETITIONER	The person filing the petition. This is you (and any co-petitioners).
"EILEEN"	Refers to EILEEN PARKER, a non-party individual who provides testimony or evidence but is not a party to the case

Note: A list of the most common party labels used in probate petitions and explains when each one should be used. Should be applied consistently throughout your filing.

Once you've introduced a person or entity this way, you should refer to them by their defined label consistently. For example, you would use "PETITIONERS" instead of repeating the full names of JOHN DOE and MARY SMITH each time. Likewise, once JANE DOE is introduced as the DECEDENT, that label should be used throughout the document when referencing her.

You can also define labels for *non-party individuals* who play a role in the facts. For instance, a witness, family member, or third-party declarant. If EILEEN PARKER provided a declaration, you might refer to her as ("EILEEN") and then use that label throughout. Consistency in these labels is not only professional, but it's essential for readability.

The terms "SETTLOR" or "TRUSTOR" are also sometimes used in petitions. These refer to the person who created the trust. When describing events that occurred while that person was alive, such as signing the trust, you may use SETTLOR. Once the person has passed away, it is more appropriate to use DECEDENT when referring to them.

Legal labels from civil court, such as "PLAINTIFF" or "DEFENDANT," do not generally apply to probate petitions and should be avoided unless you are referencing a related civil case. Similarly, terms like "PROPONDING PARTY" and "RESPONDING PARTY" are used during the discovery phase, which will be discussed in a later volume of this guide.

Required Forms for Filing a Petition

Along with the petition, most probate courts require you to submit a few additional forms at the time of filing. While requirements may vary slightly depending on the courthouse, the general process is similar throughout California.

For example, in Los Angeles County, you generally must file the petition together with two forms: the Probate Case Cover Sheet (Form PRO-010) as required by local court rules. In cases involving proceedings, such as § 850 petitions (to recover property) or will contests under § 8250, you will also need to submit a Summons (Form DE-125).

These requirements come from *California Probate Code § 8271* and the *California Rules of Court, Rule 2.111*. The headers of these required forms are shown in Figure 10.8, *Headers for Required Court Forms*, to help you visually confirm you're using the correct documents.

Figure 10.8. Headers for Required Court Forms

Official titles and form numbers of required probate forms in Los Angeles County, including PRO-010, DE-125, DE-120, and DE-120(P).

SELF-REPRESENTED

Probate Case Cover Sheet (Form PRO-010)

The PRO-010 form provides basic information about the case, including the type of petition, names of the parties, and whether there are related matters pending (see Figure 10.9, *Probate Case Cover Sheet – PRO-010*).

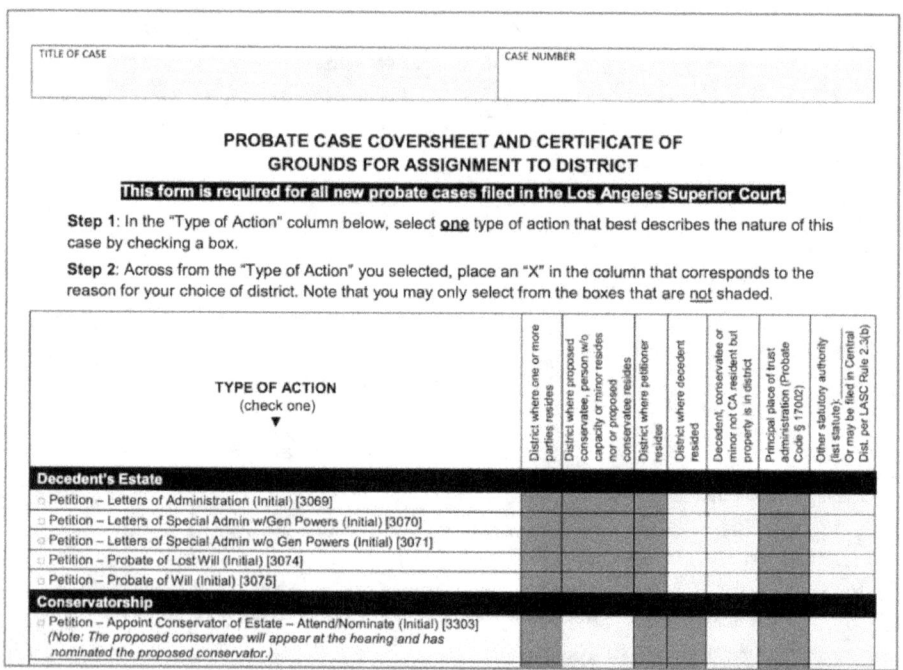

Figure 10.9. Probate Case Cover Sheet – PRO-010
For identification purposes. Use this reference to confirm you are using the correct form. Complete according to your case and local court rules.

This form ensures that your petition is routed to the correct department and properly recorded by the clerk's office. The *Summons* is the official court notice that informs the opposing party that a petition has been filed. Once you submit these forms, along with the petition, the clerk will assign a case number, stamp

188

your documents, and sign the Summons. These documents will then be returned to you.

Pay close attention to the following lines in PRO-010 to ensure accuracy:

- **Line 1: Case Number** - Leave this blank; the court will fill it in.
- **Line 3: Title of the Case** - Enter the case title exactly as it appears on your petition.
- **Line 5: Petitioner's Information** - Include your full name, address, and contact information.
- **Line 7: Nature of the Case** - Select only one box that corresponds to your type of petition (e.g., trust dispute, will contest).
- **Line 9: Related Cases** - Indicate whether there are any other ongoing related cases.

> **Tip:** Make sure all the information matches your petition to avoid delays.

Summons (Form DE-125)

The DE-125 form serves as the official court notice to inform the opposing party that a petition has been filed. Properly completing this form ensures that everyone entitled to notice is informed of the proceedings (see Figure 10.10. *Summons Form – DE-125*).

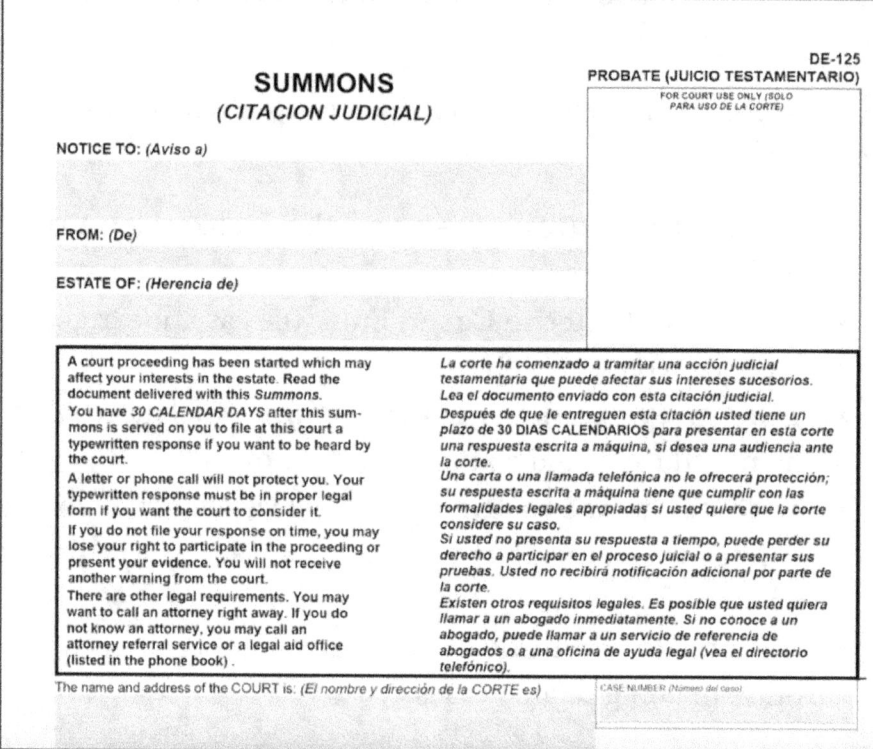

Figure 10.10. Summons Form – DE-125
Serves as the official court notice to the opposing party that a petition has been filed. Must be served along with the petition and notice of hearing to all required parties.

Note: The DE-125 Summons is generally used for petitions that function like civil lawsuits, such as **§850 petitions to recover property** or **will contests under §8250**. For most trust petitions under Probate Code §17200, you will instead use a

Notice of Hearing (Form DE-120) to notify interested parties.

When filling out DE-125, pay close attention to the following lines:

- **Line 1: Case Number** - Leave this blank; the court will complete it.
- **Line 3: Title of the Case** - Use the title exactly as shown on your petition.
- **Line 5: Hearing Date and Time** - Leave these blank; the court will fill them in when your petition is filed.
- **Line 7: Court Address** - Enter the full address of the probate division where you are filing.
- **Line 9: Petitioner's Attorney** - If you're representing yourself, write "In Pro Per" after your name.
- **Line 11: Clerk's Signature** - This section will be completed by the court when the Summons is issued.

Next Steps After Filing

Once you submit these forms along with your petition, the clerk will assign a case number, stamp your documents, and sign the Summons. These documents will then be returned to you. The next step is to notify all interested parties. To do this, you must also complete and serve a Notice of Hearing (Form DE-120), which states the date, time, and location of the hearing.

The requirement to notify interested parties is outlined in *California Probate Code § 1215*. The documents that must be served together are: the stamped petition; the signed Summons

(DE-125), if filing an § 850 petition or a § 8250 will contest; and the Notice of Hearing (DE-120). These must be delivered according to legal service rules, either by mail or personal service, depending on the circumstances and court instructions.

Notice of Hearing (Form DE-120)

The DE-120 form notifies all interested parties of the upcoming hearing, which states the date, time, and location of the hearing (see Figure 10.11, *Notice of Hearing – DE-120*). Accurate completion is essential for proper notice.

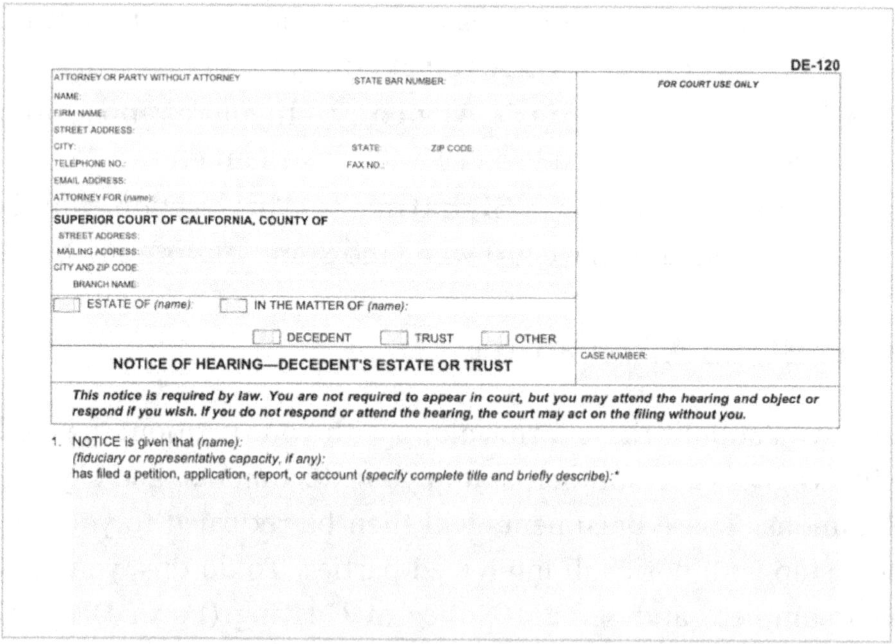

DE-120

ATTORNEY OR PARTY WITHOUT ATTORNEY STATE BAR NUMBER:
NAME:
FIRM NAME:
STREET ADDRESS:
CITY: STATE: ZIP CODE:
TELEPHONE NO.: FAX NO.:
EMAIL ADDRESS:
ATTORNEY FOR *(name)*:

FOR COURT USE ONLY

SUPERIOR COURT OF CALIFORNIA, COUNTY OF
STREET ADDRESS:
MAILING ADDRESS:
CITY AND ZIP CODE:
BRANCH NAME:

☐ ESTATE OF *(name)*: ☐ IN THE MATTER OF *(name)*:

☐ DECEDENT ☐ TRUST ☐ OTHER

NOTICE OF HEARING—DECEDENT'S ESTATE OR TRUST

CASE NUMBER:

This notice is required by law. You are not required to appear in court, but you may attend the hearing and object or respond if you wish. If you do not respond or attend the hearing, the court may act on the filing without you.

1. NOTICE is given that *(name)*:
(fiduciary or representative capacity, if any):
has filed a petition, application, report, or account *(specify complete title and briefly describe)*:*

Figure 10.11. Notice of Hearing Form – DE-120
Notifies all interested parties of the court date, time, and petition type. Must be completed and served correctly to avoid delays.

Pay close attention to the following lines in DE-120 to ensure accuracy:

- **Line 1: Case Number** - Use the number assigned to your case.
- **Line 3: Name of Decedent or Trust** - Match the name as shown on your petition.
- **Line 5: Hearing Information** - Enter the date, time, and courtroom number as provided by the court.
- **Line 7: Description of Petition** - Briefly describe the nature of your petition (e.g., "Petition to Remove Trustee and Appoint Successor").
- **Line 9: Petitioner's Contact Information** - List your full name, address, and phone number.
- **Line 11: Signature** - Sign and date the form before filing.

Proof of Service (Form DE-120(P) or POS-030)

Once service is complete, the person who served the documents must fill out a Proof of Personal Service (Form DE-120(P)), or Proof of Service by Mail (POS-030). This step is required by *California Probate Code § 1220*. The Proof of Service confirms that legal notice has been properly provided and must list the exact documents that were served, such as "Petition to Invalidate a Trust," "Summons (DE-125)," and "Notice of Hearing (DE-120)" (See Figure 10.12, *Proof of Service – DE-120(P)*).

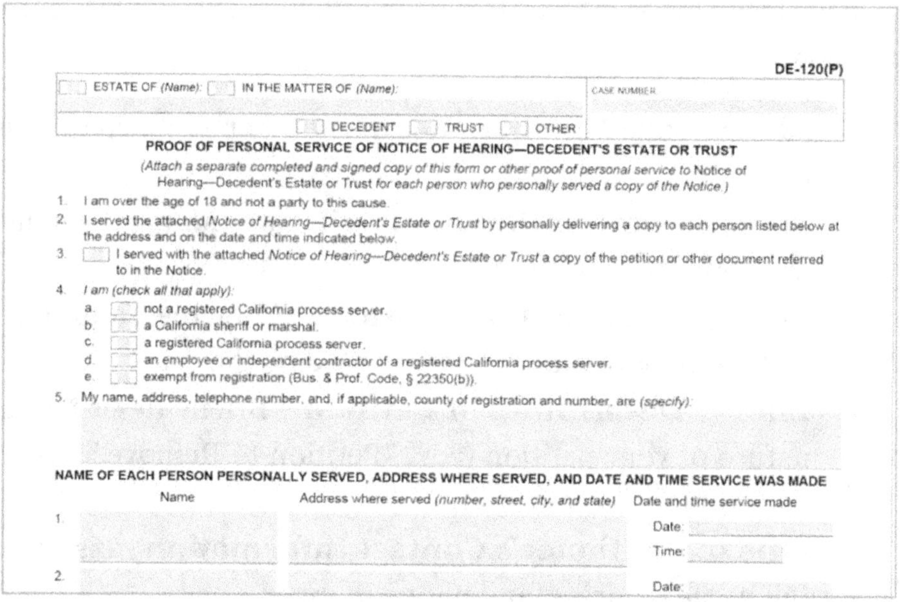

DE-120(P)

☐ ESTATE OF *(Name):* ☐ IN THE MATTER OF *(Name):*

CASE NUMBER

☐ DECEDENT ☐ TRUST ☐ OTHER

PROOF OF PERSONAL SERVICE OF NOTICE OF HEARING—DECEDENT'S ESTATE OR TRUST

(Attach a separate completed and signed copy of this form or other proof of personal service to Notice of Hearing—Decedent's Estate or Trust *for each person who personally served a copy of the Notice.)*

1. I am over the age of 18 and not a party to this cause.
2. I served the attached *Notice of Hearing—Decedent's Estate or Trust* by personally delivering a copy to each person listed below at the address and on the date and time indicated below.
3. ☐ I served with the attached *Notice of Hearing—Decedent's Estate or Trust* a copy of the petition or other document referred to in the Notice.
4. *I am (check all that apply):*
   a. ☐ not a registered California process server.
   b. ☐ a California sheriff or marshal.
   c. ☐ a registered California process server.
   d. ☐ an employee or independent contractor of a registered California process server.
   e. ☐ exempt from registration (Bus. & Prof. Code, § 22350(b)).
5. My name, address, telephone number, and, if applicable, county of registration and number, are *(specify):*

NAME OF EACH PERSON PERSONALLY SERVED, ADDRESS WHERE SERVED, AND DATE AND TIME SERVICE WAS MADE

	Name	Address where served *(number, street, city, and state)*	Date and time service made
1.			Date: Time:
2.			Date:

Figure 10.12. Proof of Service Form DE-120(P)
Confirms notice was served to all required parties. Must be completed by a neutral third party and filed with the court.

It's crucial to note that the person who completes and signs the Proof of Service cannot be a party to the case. For example, the petitioner or any other interested party. Instead, service must be performed by a neutral third party who is at least 18 years old. This can include a spouse, neighbor, friend, or any other adult who is not directly involved in the case.

Alternatively, you can take the documents to the courthouse and request that they be served by the **county sheriff**. Many sheriff's departments offer this service for a fee, and they will complete the **Proof of Service** on your behalf. This option can be particularly useful if the opposing party is difficult to locate or is known to avoid service.

When filling out DE-120(p), pay close attention to the following lines:

- **Line 1: Case Number** - Match the number on your petition.
- **Line 3: Name of Decedent or Trust** - Be consistent with your other forms.
- **Line 5: Method of Service** - Indicate whether you served by mail, in person, or other approved methods.
- **Line 7: Server's Name** - Enter the full name of the person who served the documents (cannot be you if you are a party).
- **Line 9: Documents Served** - Clearly list each document (e.g., "Petition to Invalidate Trust," "Summons (DE-125)," "Notice of Hearing (DE-120)").
- **Line 11: Declaration of Service** - The server must sign and date this section under penalty of perjury.

After the Proof of Service is completed and signed, you must file it with the court along with the Notice of Hearing (DE-120). This confirms that service was completed according to the legal requirements outlined in *California Probate Code §§ 1219–1220*.

Final Step: Returning to Court

After the documents have been served and the Proof of Service (DE-120(P) or POS-030) is completed and signed, you must return to the court and file two things: the Notice of Hearing (DE-120) and the Proof of Service (DE-120(P) or POS-030). This confirms that service was completed in compliance with California Probate Code §§ 1219–1220.

Each form has a specific role in ensuring the proper processing of your probate petition (see Table 10.3, *Required Probate Forms (California)*).

Table 10.3. Required Probate Forms (California)

Form No.	Form Name	Purpose	When Filed
PRO-010	Probate Case Cover Sheet	Identifies case info; helps clerk route petition properly	Initial filing
DE-125	Summons	Court-issued notice after petition is filed	Initial filing
DE-120	Notice of Hearing	Notifies interested parties of court date and time	After service, second filing
DE-120(P)	Proof of Service	Verifies documents were served correctly and legally	After service, second filing

Note. This table outlines standard forms required when filing a probate petition in California, including their purpose and typical filing stage.

For a visual timeline, see **Figure 11.2** refer to **Chapter 11**.

> **Tip: Organize and Keep Everything.** Make copies of every form you file, receive, or serve-digitally and in print. Keep them in chronological order, with labels or notes if needed. Courts often request re- submission of documents, and being able to quickly retrieve proof of filing or service can prevent delays or confusion. Treat your case like a case file- because that's what it is.

Verification: Why It Matters and How to Draft It

In probate cases, most petitions, responses, and other court filings must include a **verification**. A verification is a formal statement signed under penalty of perjury, confirming that the information in the document is true to the best of your knowledge. It assures the court that you are swearing the facts presented are accurate and complete.

Why Verification Is Required

The purpose of a verification is to add a layer of accountability. By signing, you affirm that the statements made in your petition are not only accurate but also made in good faith. Failing to include a verification when required may result in your filing being rejected or delayed. The court needs to know that the information you are presenting is credible and that you take responsibility for its truthfulness.

Where to Include the Verification

Typically, the verification appears at the end of your petition or supplemental filing, just before your signature. It is presented on a separate page and formatted similarly to a declaration. Label the page **"Verification"** at the top and follow your court's formatting rules.

What to Include in a Verification

A proper verification contains a short, legally binding statement confirming the truth of your filing. It is signed under penalty of perjury and helps ensure the integrity of the court process.

A standard verification includes the following elements (see *Figure 10.13. Example of Verification Statement*):

> **VERIFICATION**
>
> I, [Your Full Name], declare as follows:
>
> I am the Petitioner in this proceeding. I have read the [Insert Title of Document] and know its contents. The matters stated in the foregoing document are true of my own knowledge, except as to those matters which are stated on information and belief, and as to those matters, I believe them to be true.
>
> I declare under penalty of perjury under the laws of the State of California that the foregoing is true and correct.
>
> Executed on [insert date], at [insert city], California.
>
> Respectfully submitted,
>
> _____
>
> [Your Full Name], Petitioner

Figure 10.13. Example of Verification Statement
Standard format confirming the petition's truthfulness under penalty of perjury, including signature, date, and location.

To create a proper verification, include:

- **Your name and role**, such as "Petitioner" or "Objector."
- **A statement confirming that you've read the petition** and believe the facts stated in it are true and correct.
- **A penalty of perjury clause**, such as:
- *"I declare under penalty of perjury under the laws of the State of California that the foregoing is true and correct."*
- **Your signature, the date, and the location** (city and state) where you signed it.

This simple paragraph usually goes at the end of your petition. Do not leave it out—without it, the court may reject your filing.

Signature Requirements: Wet vs. Electronic Signatures

Most courts require petitions to be signed under penalty of perjury, meaning the petitioner affirms that all statements in the document are true to the best of their knowledge. This requirement is governed by *California Code of Civil Procedure § 2015.5*. The petitioner must always sign the petition. In cases where the petitioner is represented by an attorney, the attorney may also be required to sign certain parts of the filing.

There are two primary types of signatures accepted by the court: wet signatures and electronic signatures. A **wet signature** is a traditional, handwritten signature signed in ink. If you are filing electronically in a court that permits eFiling (such as Los Angeles), the signed document may be scanned and submitted through the court's eFiling system. Alternatively, **electronic signatures** may be used under specific conditions outlined in *California Rules of Court, Rule 2.257* (see Figure 10.14, *Comparison of Wet and Electronic Signatures*).

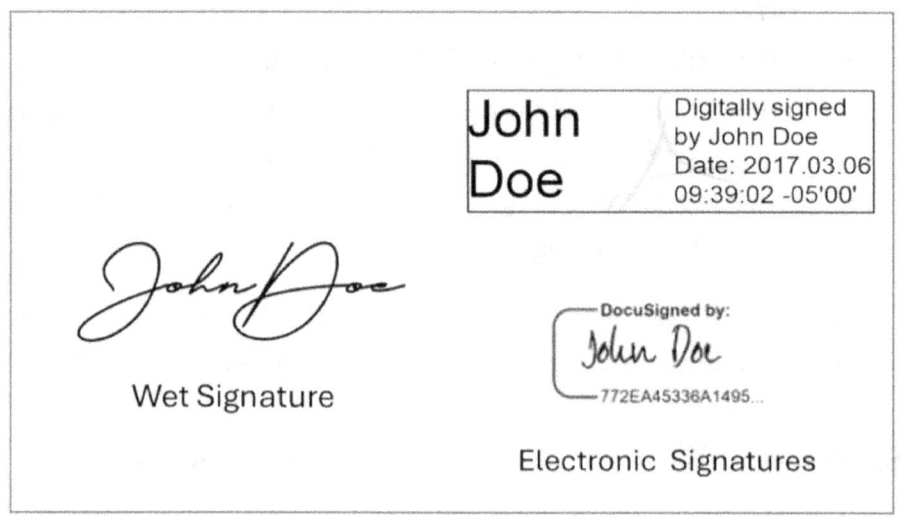

Figure 10.14 Comparison of Wet and Electronic Signatures
A sample wet signature on the left—a traditional handwritten signature in ink—and two forms of electronic signatures on the right. The first is generated using Adobe Sign, and the second is created through DocuSign.

According to Rule 2.257, a document submitted under penalty of perjury is considered signed if the signer has done one of the following: (1) Electronically signed the document using a verifiable and secure method, or (2) Physically signed a printed version of the document prior to filing.

If the second method is used, the person submitting the electronic version must retain the original signed copy and produce it upon request. This rule allows for flexibility: some courts accept typed names (for example, /s/ JOHN DOE. This format should be typed exactly as shown, including the forward slashes) as a valid electronic signature, while others may require that the signature be uniquely identifiable, under the signer's sole control, and verifiable.

In practice, this means that drawing a signature with a stylus or using a signature field in a PDF may be acceptable for many filings. However, courts generally do not accept photocopied or incomplete signatures on documents that require verification. Los Angeles Superior Court follows Rule 2.257 and has confirmed in its General Order re Mandatory Electronic Filing that all e-Filed documents submitted under penalty of perjury must comply with these requirements.

Petitioners should always confirm whether electronic signatures are permitted in their court and whether the type of signature being used meets the verification and retention standards set out in Rule 2.257. Failure to comply may result in a rejected filing.

By understanding and following these signature rules, petitioners can ensure their documents are valid, complete, and ready for court review.

Organizing and Managing Your Documents

Staying organized is crucial when navigating a probate case—especially when preparing, filing, and tracking multiple documents. A well-structured system will help you keep track of important paperwork, avoid duplicate efforts, and ensure you have everything you need when the court requests it.

Keep Copies of Everything

As you begin filing and serving documents, make it a habit to keep copies of everything. Whether printed or digital, maintain a complete record that includes:

- Your petition and any amendments
- All required forms (e.g., PRO-010; DE-125, if required; DE-120; and DE-120(P) or POS-030)
- Court-stamped copies
- Proofs of service
- Court receipts and filing confirmations
- Mailing and delivery confirmations

Keep Key Documents Within Reach

Throughout my case, I found it helpful to keep certain documents printed and always within reach. I created a **quick-reference folder** that I could easily flip through whenever needed. This folder included:

1. The Living Trust and Will
2. My original Petition
3. A one-page Case Summary taped to the front of my binder, which included:
   a. Case Number and Case Name (exactly how it's recorded on the court's website)
   b. Petitioner's names
   c. Respondent's name
   d. Respondent's Attorney's address and phone number
   e. Contact information for all parties

Having this quick-access information saved me time—especially when I needed to make a phone call, reference a document, or fill out a new form.

Digital Document Management

For most of my documents, I preferred saving them electronically. I used Dropbox, a free cloud-based program that allowed me to access the documents from anywhere, anytime. This also ensured that my files were safely stored even if my computer crashed or got lost.

File Naming and Version Control

Organizing your digital files systematically is essential for quick and accurate access. I recommend giving each document a clear title, a date to indicate the version, and a status marker to show its stage in the filing process. This way, you'll always know which version is the most recent and what it represents.

Here's the file-naming format I used to keep versions organized and easy to find:

DocumentTitle_Date_Status.extension (Date: MMDDYY)

> **Author's Tip: Filing Name Examples**
>
> Using a consistent naming convention helped me quickly identify the status and purpose of each document.
>
> Here are some examples:
>
> - **Petition2Invalidate_041225.docx** (draft version before signing and filing)
>
> - **Petition2Invalidate_041525_Signed.pdf** (signed version, ready for filing)
>
> - **Petition2Invalidate_042025_CourtApproved.pdf** (approved and returned by the court)
>
> - **Supplement2ClearNotes_051025.docx** (final draft of the supplement, ready for submission)
>
> - **Supplement2ClearNotes_051025.pdf** (final PDF of the supplement, submitted to the court)
>
> - **Objection2Will_060125.pdf** (objection after filing, reflecting court acknowledgment)
>
> By consistently including the document title, date, and status in the file name, I could quickly find what I needed—especially when managing multiple versions or updates.

Note: For single-digit months or days, I include a leading zero to avoid confusion. For example, writing the date as **011225** clearly indicates **January 12, 2025**. If I wrote **11225** instead, it could be misinterpreted as **November 2, 2025**. Using a zero ensures that the date format is consistent and easy to read.

This naming system makes it clear which version is the most recent and what stage the document is in. You may also want to use descriptors like _Final, _Amended, or _Served to make tracking easier. Personally, I found that following this system (even if not perfectly) made it much easier to locate documents quickly. Whenever I needed to reference a specific file, I could do so without wasting time searching through folders. It also gave me peace of mind knowing that I could easily identify the latest version of each document.

Use Folders to Stay Organized

On my computer, I created separate folders for each significant step or filing (see Figure 10.15, *Example of an Organized Filing System*, such as:

- Discovery
- Evidence
- HearingNotice_ServiceProofs
- Motion4Financial Accounting
- MSC
- Petition2Invalidate
- ProbateNotes_Supplements
- Subpoena
- Will Contest

Figure 10.15. Example of an Organized Filing System
A structured folder system helps keep probate documents clear and accessible. Use consistent names, subfolders, and dates to simplify tracking and prep.

Within each folder, I saved related documents in chronological order, using file names that reflected the date and content (Figure 10.15. This structure made it easy to locate specific documents when preparing for hearings or responding to court requests.

Managing Physical Copies

Even though I maintained digital files, I still had physical copies that I had to keep organized. It's important to keep hard copies of the most essential documents. Use a large, durable 3-ring binder with labeled tabs to separate:

- Filed petitions and court-stamped copies
- Proofs of service and mailing receipts
- Court notices and rulings
- Copies of correspondence with the opposing party
- Key financial and medical records

This was in addition to the dedicated folder near my workspace with the most frequently needed documents—especially the Living Trust, Pour-Over Will, original Petition, and the Title Page on paper. This folder was invaluable when I needed quick access without digging through my larger binder.

Digital Quick-Access Page

In addition to the printed reference materials, I created a single **electronic document** titled **"Title Page"** on my computer desktop. This pre-filled document included information that never changed: our names and addresses, the respondent's name, the case name, and the case number. I also added the verification page with signature lines.

To make updating easier, I highlighted the areas that needed changes, such as the document name on both the title page and verification page, as well as dates. This setup allowed me to quickly update and print the document whenever I needed it, saving time with each new filing. Keeping it on my desktop meant I didn't have to search through folders every time I needed a fresh copy.

Backup and Security

To protect your files from loss or damage, create backups on an external hard drive or a secure cloud storage service. Regularly update your backups and consider setting up automatic syncing for your digital folders. Use strong, unique passwords to protect sensitive files, and avoid storing them on shared or public computers.

Stay Consistent

Whatever system you choose, stick with it. Consistency will make it easier to find documents quickly and reduce stress when preparing for court. The more organized you are from the beginning, the less likely you are to lose track of important records as the case progresses.

By keeping your documents orderly and secure, you'll save time, reduce frustration, and be better prepared for each stage of the probate process.

Conclusion

Ensuring that your petition is properly formatted, signed, and submitted is crucial for court acceptance. This chapter has covered the essential procedural requirements for California probate, particularly focusing on formatting, supporting documents, and required forms.

Although California's probate procedures are uniquely complex, the principles outlined here, such as clear formatting, proper filing, and including necessary exhibits, are useful in most jurisdictions. Always check your local court rules to ensure compliance.

In the next chapter, we'll move from procedural requirements to legal content. You'll learn how to craft a petition that meets court standards while also presenting a clear, persuasive argument.

Meeting procedural requirements is crucial to getting your petition accepted by the court. The following highlights the most important formatting, filing, and documentation guidelines from this chapter (see Figure 10.16, *Key Takeaways – Technical Requirements*).

1. Proper formatting and adherence to procedural rules are crucial for your petition's acceptance in probate court.
2. Pleading Paper: Use 28-line numbered paper with standard margins, formatted according to California Rules of Court.
3. Title Page: Include the petitioner's information, court name, case number (left blank), and a clear petition title with applicable Probate Code sections.
4. Formatting the Petition: Use a hierarchical heading structure for clarity and follow paragraph numbering and indentation guidelines.
5. Signature Requirements: Check whether wet or electronic signatures are accepted and follow rules for electronic filing under *Rule 2.257*.
6. Supporting Documents: Include core documents like the contested trust or will, medical records, or financial statements as exhibits, labeled and referenced properly.
7. Filing and Service: Complete necessary forms (such as the Probate Case Cover Sheet and Summons) and follow up with proper service and proof of service.
8. While your petition isn't perfect, following procedural guidelines may improve your chances of court acceptance.

Figure 10.16. Key Takeaways – Technical Requirements
Covers key procedural rules for probate petitions—formatting, signatures, supporting docs, and filing. Following these helps meet court standards and avoid rejection.

CHAPTER 11

The Final Step: Filing Your Petition

Introduction

Filing a petition correctly is only the first step in the legal process. To ensure that the court accepts the petition and moves the case forward, the petitioner must carefully review their documents for accuracy, assemble the filing packet, submit the petition, and properly serve notice to all required parties. This chapter provides a step-by-step guide to completing the filing process, avoiding delays, and ensuring all procedural requirements are met.

In most cases, you must file your petition in the county where the decedent resided at the time of death, as this determines the proper jurisdiction for probate matters. However, if your petition involves a trust, you may also be able to file in the county where the trust is administered. Filing in the wrong county can result in delays or even dismissal of your case. Always call your local probate court to confirm the correct venue before filing.

Final Review Before Filing

Before submitting the petition, a thorough final review is essential to ensure that all technical, procedural, and legal requirements have been met. If the court finds that your petition is incomplete or improperly formatted, they will typically issue a notice of rejection or a list of deficiencies. You will then have to correct the issues and resubmit your documents, which can cause significant delays.

To avoid this, start by checking for **technical compliance**: make sure the document follows the correct formatting guidelines, contains all required sections, and is structured correctly with numbered paragraphs and exhibits.

Next, verify the **legal content** to confirm that claims are clearly stated, your legal arguments are strong, and you have sufficient supporting evidence. The petition should be reviewed to ensure that it effectively presents the petitioner's case, citing relevant probate laws where applicable. Additionally, all required attachments and exhibits should be accounted for, including declarations, financial records, medical reports, and any supporting documents that strengthen the case.

Another crucial step is verifying that all **signatures are complete**. Most courts require petitions to be signed under penalty of perjury. In e-filing courts, a wet signature (signed in ink) can be scanned and submitted electronically, or you may use an electronic signature, such as a typed name or drawn signature. According to California Rules of Court, Rule 2.257, either method is acceptable as long as the signature is unique to the signer, under their sole control, and capable of verification. Always check your local court's e-filing guidelines to ensure compliance and keep the original signed document on file in case it is requested.

I once had a supplement rejected because the title on my document didn't exactly match the title on the required form. Fortunately, I was able to fix it and resubmit without further issue. This experience taught me the importance of double-checking every detail before filing—especially when it comes to matching court forms precisely.

Author's Tip

Before you file, have someone review your petition or declaration—preferably someone who isn't emotionally involved in the case.

- ❖ Does it make sense to someone unfamiliar with your situation?
- ❖ Does it clearly and honestly reflect what happened?
- ❖ Does it support your legal claims with facts—not just feelings?

Filing a court document means you're swearing it's true. A fresh set of eyes can help catch errors, unclear language, emotional tone, or weak reasoning that may hurt your case.

Take a breath. Reread it. Be sure.

Assembling the Filing Packet

Once the petition and supporting documents have been finalized, they must be organized into a complete filing packet to prevent processing delays. The main petition serves as the core document and should be placed at the front of the packet. In addition to the petition, most courts require specific forms such as cover sheets, verification statements, and declarations. These documents should be arranged in the order required by the court to ensure efficient processing.

If you are filing electronically (e-filing), you will typically upload each document separately, rather than as a single packet. Make sure to properly label each file according to the court's instructions, as incorrect labeling can lead to processing errors or rejection. Check your local court's e-filing guidelines to ensure compliance.

Supporting evidence must also be included in the filing packet. Exhibits, such as financial records, medical reports, and witness declarations, should be clearly labeled and properly referenced within the petition. All exhibits should be attached to the back of your petition rather than submitting them as separate documents. This ensures that the petition and its supporting evidence are treated as a single, cohesive document.

If the petitioner is requesting a fee waiver, the required forms and supporting financial documents must be included as well.

Before filing, the petitioner should prepare multiple copies of the entire filing packet. The original will be submitted to the court, but additional copies are needed for personal records and for serving notice to all required parties.

If filing a physical copy, make printed copies ahead of time, as the court may not provide duplicates. If filing an electronic copy (e-filing), save the file-stamped PDF immediately after submission. Regardless of the method, keeping at least one file-stamped copy for your records is strongly recommended, as it serves as proof of submission in case any questions or issues arise later.

Final Review Before Filing

Before you submit your petition, use the **Filing Checklist** to make sure everything is complete and in order. This tool walks you through the last steps to help you file confidently and avoid preventable delays.

> **Final Review Before Filing.** Download the **Filing Checklist** to ensure you have everything in order at https://properprobate.guide/california-filing or scan the QR code. It walks you through every detail to make certain your petition is complete and accurate before your first court appearance.

Filing Methods & Logistics (How & Where to File Your Petition)

Once the petition is finalized and signed, it must be formally submitted to the probate court. California courts offer multiple filing methods, each with its own rules and requirements. The method used (electronic, in-person, or by mail) will depend on your county's procedures.

In many counties, including Los Angeles, probate petitions must be submitted electronically using an approved Electronic Filing Service Provider (EFSP). E-filing allows the petitioner to upload documents online, receive instant confirmation of submission, and track their case electronically. E-filing is

governed by *California Rules of Court, rules 2.250–2.261*, which outline formatting and signature requirements for electronically filed documents. Los Angeles Superior Court mandates e-filing for most probate documents and maintains an up-to-date list of approved EFSPs at:
https://www.lacourt.org/division/efiling/providers.aspx

The petitioner can choose from any EFSP listed on the court's site, including popular platforms like One Legal, File & ServeXpress, and LegalConnect. Each provider charges a small service fee in addition to the court's regular filing fee.

> **Tip: Pay Attention to Court File-Naming Rules.** Many courts have unique file-naming conventions that must be followed when submitting documents electronically. These may include specifying the case number, document type, and date in a particular format. Failure to use the correct naming conventions can result in rejected filings or processing delays. Always check your court's e- filing guidelines to ensure your file names comply with local requirements.

If the court permits **in-person filing**, the petitioner must bring two copies of the filing packet: the original and a copy. The court will keep the original for their records and file-stamp the copy before returning it to you. To ensure you have enough copies for serving notice to interested parties, it's a good idea to bring a few extra copies as well. Some courts allow in-person filing only for self-represented litigants or under limited circumstances, so always check your local court's website or call the probate division clerk in advance.

If filing by mail, it's recommended to use a tracking method such as USPS Certified Mail. You should include both the original and a copy in your mailing. The court will keep the original and file-stamp the copy, then return it to you. Be sure to include a self-addressed, stamped envelope (SASE) so the court can send back the file-stamped copy. Before mailing your petition, confirm you have the correct probate division address by checking your county court's official website.

Most probate petitions require a filing fee, which is currently $435 in California (subject to local surcharges). If the petitioner cannot afford the fee, they may request a waiver by filing *Form FW-001* (Request to Waive Court Fees) and *Form FW-003* (Order on Court Fee Waiver). Fee waiver policies are based on *Government Code § 68630 et seq.* and *California Rules of Court, rule 3.55*. Documentation such as proof of income or public assistance eligibility is usually required. The court must approve the request before the petitioner can proceed without payment.

Once your petition is filed, the court will assign a case number. This number is used for all future documents and for tracking case updates. The case number must appear on all future documents. Many courts offer online case access so you can check updates, confirm hearing dates, and view filed documents. After filing, your next required step will be serving notice to all interested parties.

Serving the Other Party

Before your case can move forward, the law requires that you notify all interested parties about your petition. This step, called

service of notice, meaning the formal delivery of legal documents to inform involved parties of the court proceedings, is not just a courtesy; it's a legal requirement designed to give everyone who might be affected by the outcome a chance to respond. If notice is not given properly, your petition may be delayed, continued, or even dismissed by the court.

The list of people who must be served depends on the nature of your petition. In most trust-related matters, this includes the acting trustee, all current and remainder beneficiaries, any named successor trustees, and often legal heirs—especially if your petition challenges the trust's validity or changes who will receive assets. If the trustee previously mailed a Administration under Probate Code § 16061.7, anyone who received that notice is generally considered an interested party and should be served with your petition.

When I first started the process, I thought the law literally meant "everyone" should be served. So, I kept sending documents to my brother and his attorney. Eventually, his attorney called to tell me to stop sending documents directly to my brother. Since my brother had legal representation, I needed to send everything to the attorney instead. He also explained that if I ever got an attorney, I should let him know, because at that point, it would no longer be proper for him to communicate with me directly. This experience taught me that when someone has an attorney, all communications, including serving documents, must go through their attorney.

When in doubt, it's safer to serve more people than fewer. Some courts expect the petitioner to serve everyone named in the trust, even if those individuals are not directly impacted by the petition. In rare cases, such as petitions involving charitable trusts, unclaimed property, or unknown heirs, the California Attorney General, the state's chief legal officer responsible for representing the public's interest, may also need to be notified.

Service is usually completed by mail, not personal delivery. Unlike civil lawsuits, where personal service is often required, probate allows notice to be served by first-class mail (Probate Code § 1215), as long as the person serving the documents is at least 18 years old and not a party to the case. Some petitioners choose to use certified mail with return receipt for added peace of mind, though it is not required. Personal delivery is permitted but not typically necessary unless ordered by the court.

If you cannot locate a required party despite making a good-faith effort, you may request permission from the court to serve by publication, which involves publishing notice in a legal newspaper. However, this requires prior court approval through a formal Declaration of Due Diligence and is not usually applicable for most trust petitions.

Courts impose strict deadlines for serving notice. In California, the required parties must generally be served at least 30 days before the hearing. If you miss this deadline, the court may issue a probate note, continue the hearing, or take the matter off calendar until notice is correctly completed.

Optional: Include a Table of Recipients

If your case involves several parties, such as multiple beneficiaries, heirs, or successor trustees, it can be helpful to include a separate page summarizing who was served, their role in the trust or estate, and the address used for service (see Figure 11.1, *Service Summary List*). This summary is not legally required, but it may make your filing easier for the court and opposing counsel to review. In my case, the respondent's attorney added a table, so I added one too. I believe it showed the court I was being transparent and thorough.

```
                         SERVICE SUMMARY
         The following parties were served as required:
              Name (relationship to decedent)        Mailing Address
              John Doe (son)                         123 Main Street
                                                     Pasadena, CA 91106

              Mary Doe Smith (daughter)              456 Elm Street
                                                     Los Angeles, CA 90042

              David Doe (son)                        789 Cedar Lane
                                                     South Pasadena, CA 91030

              Eileen Paker (Successor Trustee)       654 Maple Drive
                                                     Sacramento, CA 94023

              Robert Baker (Respondent's Attorney)   321 Park Avenue
                                                     Woodland Hills, CA 91365
```

Figure 11.1. Service Summary List
This list provides the names, relationships, and mailing addresses of individuals served in connection with the petition. Clearly presenting this information helps the court and opposing counsel verify that notice was properly given to all relevant parties.

You can format your table simply, listing the person's name, their role (e.g., trustee, remainder beneficiary), and the full mailing address where notice was sent. Title the page something like "Service Summary Table" and include it behind the Proof of Service form or as a supplemental filing (Figure. Judges and clerks appreciate anything that helps them quickly verify that legal notice was given to the correct people.

Filing Proof of Service with the Court

Once service has been completed, the petitioner must file a **Proof of Service** form with the court. This document confirms that all legally required parties were notified, and that service was completed correctly. The specific form you use depends on how service was carried out. For example, service by mail, personal delivery, or publication. Submitting the correct form is essential, as failure to do so can delay the case or result in it being taken off calendar.

One of the most common mistakes in probate cases is simply forgetting to file the Proof of Service. Even if you serve all the right people at the right time, the court cannot proceed without documented proof. Other common errors include serving parties too late, using a method not permitted by law, or failing to include details such as the server's name, the date of service, or the method used.

Three forms are typically involved in this process:

1. **Summons (Form DE-125):** Filed alongside the initial petition when the petition functions like a civil action, such as probate code § 850 to recover property, or a will contest under § 8250. This form formally notifies the respondent or interested parties that a legal action has been filed and that they are required to respond. After it is submitted, the court clerk signs the summons and returns it to the petitioner for personal service.

2. **Notice of Hearing (Form DE-120)**: This document provides the date, time, and location of the upcoming court hearing. After the court sets a hearing date, the petitioner must serve the Notice of Hearing, along with the stamped petition and, if required, signed summons, on all interested parties. Although this form is not filed immediately, it must be included later as part of the proof of service submission.

3. **Proof of Personal Service (Form DE-120(P)** or **Mail Service (POS-030)**, which is completed and signed by the person who performed the service. This form details who was served, how the documents were delivered, and when service occurred. After completing service, the petitioner must file this form along with a copy of the signed summons and any additional documents (like a service table, if one was included) to demonstrate full compliance.

How the Forms Work Together

To summarize (see Figure 11.2, *Step-by-Step Guide to Filing and Service a Probate Petition*):

Step 1: The petitioner begins by filing the *Petition*, *Probate Case Cover Sheet (Form PRO-010)*, and, if the case requires it (such as under § 850) the *Summons (Form DE-125)*. The court stamps the petition, signs the summons, and returns them for service.

Step 2: The petitioner serves the stamped petition, signed summons (if applicable), and *Notice of Hearing (Form DE-120)* on all required parties.

Step 3: Once service is complete, the person who served the documents fills out and signs the *Proof of Service* form.

Step 4: The petitioner then files the *signed Proof of Service* and copies of any *signed* **summons** with the court.

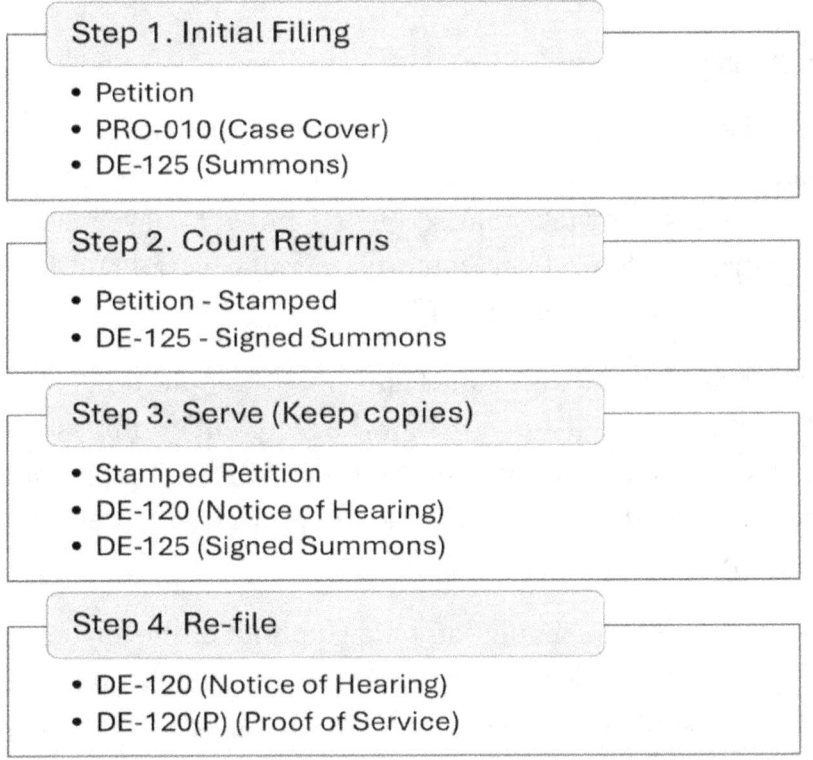

Figure 11.2. Step-by-Step Guide to Filing and Serving a Probate Petition
The two key stages of the probate petition process: (1) filing your initial documents with the court—including Summons (Form DE-125) if required by the type of petition—and (2) completing service and

filing additional forms after a hearing date is assigned. It clarifies which documents are submitted at the start and which must be served and refiled once the court sets a hearing.

By completing these steps carefully and correctly, you ensure that your case can move forward without unnecessary delays. Properly filing the Proof of Service is crucial, as the court cannot proceed without confirmation that notice was given to all relevant parties.

Our Experience

When I served my request for a formal accounting by certified mail, I thought I had done everything right. But then the respondent's attorney emailed me, claiming, "I never received any correspondence from you on December 11, 2023. Did you mail it to the correct address?"

That's when I realized something most people don't know: certified mail receipts don't show the recipient's address—only the city, zip code, and tracking number. If I had only kept the receipt, I wouldn't have had concrete proof that it went to the correct place.

Fortunately, my husband had taken a photo of the envelope at the post office, clearly showing the attorney's name and address. I sent the attorney that photo along with the USPS tracking receipt. That was the end of his claim that he hadn't received it.

The attorney only tried that tactic once.

Conclusion

Submitting a petition to probate court is more than just a bureaucratic step—it's a legal act that must meet precise standards. Each step, from organizing your documents to serving notice and filing proof, plays a critical role in whether your case is heard or stalled. Small mistakes—like using the wrong form, serving the wrong person, or forgetting to file your proof of service—can have big consequences. But with the right preparation, you can avoid those pitfalls and give your case the best chance of success. Figure 11.3 highlights the key takeaways from this chapter and serves as a final checklist to help ensure your petition is properly filed and served (see Figure 11.2, *Key Takeaways – Filing a Petition*).

> **Pro Tip:** Before you send anything by certified mail, take a picture of the envelope showing the recipient's name and address. Pair that with the receipt and tracking confirmation. It may feel excessive-but in court, it's your backup.

1. The petition must be thoroughly reviewed before filing to ensure it meets technical, legal, and procedural requirements.
2. Assemble a complete filing packet, including the petition, required court forms, supporting evidence, fee payment (or waiver), and extra copies for your records.
3. Choose the correct filing method—electronically, in person, or by mail—based on local court rules.
4. After filing, expect the court to assign a case number and issue initial instructions or deadlines.
5. Serve notice to all required parties through the appropriate method (personal service, certified mail, or publication, if necessary).
6. File Proof of Service with the court to confirm that all parties were properly notified.
7. Failure to serve notice correctly or file the Proof of Service may result in delays, continuances, or case dismissal.

Figure 11.3. Key Takeaways – Filing a Petition.
Highlights the key steps for avoiding delays or dismissal—finalizing your filing packet, serving notice, and submitting proof of service. Use this list to ensure accuracy and completeness.

Epilogue: What Happens After Filing a Petition

Filing a petition and serving notice is just the beginning of your journey through probate court. In **Volume I**, we walked through the foundational steps—how to prepare, file, and properly notify all required parties. However, once your petition is filed, the process continues with new challenges, decisions, and court appearances that can feel overwhelming.

After your petition is submitted, the court will assign a **case number** and schedule a **hearing date.** You may begin receiving **probate notes**—internal memos from the court identifying missing documents, service issues, or requests for clarification. It's your responsibility to review these notes carefully, respond appropriately, and resolve any issues before the hearing.

At the same time, opposing parties might file **objections** or even a **counter-petition**, particularly when there's a dispute over the estate's administration or the validity of the trust. Knowing how to read, understand, and respond to these filings is essential to keep your case on track.

Looking Ahead: Volume II

Volume II: Preparing for Court will guide you through everything that comes after filing, including:

- **Responding to Objections:** How to draft and file a reply when someone contests your petition.
- **Filing a Counter-Petition:** What to do if someone else files for **Letters of Administration** or disputes your claim.
- **Understanding Probate Notes:** How to read, interpret, and resolve issues raised by the court before your hearing.
- **Your First Day in Court:** What to bring, how to present yourself, and how to handle the stress of appearing before a judge.
- **Managing Court Procedures:** Topics like **continuances**, **supplements**, **case management conferences**, and more.

Moving Forward with Confidence

Whether you're representing yourself out of necessity or choice, the process can be daunting. But you're not alone. Volume II will walk with you through the next stage, offering practical advice, templates, and support to help you confidently navigate your first court appearance.

This guide was created by someone who has been through it—because I understand how confusing and isolating probate can feel when you're on your own. If this guide has been helpful, I'd love to stay connected.

To get updates on Volume II, explore free resources, or download templates, visit: www.properprobate.guide

You'll find more support, practical tools, and encouragement when you need it most.

Acknowledgements

First and foremost, to my husband, Keith, thank you for supporting me in every way that mattered. Whether it was dropping off certified mail at the post office, forwarding court emails, or simply giving me the space to disappear into my work—you never questioned my process. You understood when I needed to retreat, to focus, to go deep. *That unspoken understanding was everything.*

To my siblings, while I carried much of the load—researching, writing, filing—I never carried it alone. Your support, quick responses, and unity gave the case its strength. We stood together on truth, and because of that, *we were heard.*

To my dear friend Debbie, thank you for the weekly hikes—and your therapist's ear—for listening to every rant, every doubt, every legal twist I tried to untangle. Those walks were invaluable; *your presence, a gift.*

To my late father, your quiet perseverance lives in me. You survived the unimaginable and still carried on. That kind of grit doesn't vanish—it passes through generations. *It carried me, too.*

And to my mother, even though you're no longer with us, your presence never left me. I felt your love every step of the way—

guiding me. When I wandered off course, you nudged me back. When I felt unsteady, you anchored me.

Your love didn't just guide me—*it lit the way.*

About the Author

I am not a lawyer. I'm a university lecturer with a doctorate in education and learning technologies, specializing in research writing and activism. These skills became invaluable when I found myself navigating probate court on behalf of my siblings and me. Like many families, we didn't have the resources to hire an attorney when faced with a legal battle over my mother's estate. And while the right to represent ourselves exists, the reality is that it's an incredibly difficult road.

Fortunately, I was able to draw on my academic background and apply the same principles I teach my students: how to construct a logical argument, cite credible sources, and communicate clearly and persuasively.

In addition to research writing, I developed and teach *Activism and Environmental Justice,* a course that reflects my deep commitment to advocacy and empowerment. Whether it's fighting for environmental protections or navigating a legal system that often works against those without resources, I believe knowledge is the most powerful tool for people who feel powerless. That belief is what inspired this guide.

The probate process can be overwhelming—and for those without legal representation, it can feel impossible. My goal is to bridge that gap by offering practical tools and strategies I wish I'd had when I began.

This book is a labor of love, written with the hope that it helps even one person move through this daunting process with greater confidence. What began as a straightforward how-to quickly became something more because I couldn't ignore just how much people need to know. If this book makes the journey even slightly easier for someone, then every moment spent writing it was worth it.

A Work in Progress

This guide is a living document, and I am constantly learning. As I've said, I'm not a lawyer—just someone sharing my experience. I recognize that every case is different and that laws and procedures continue to evolve.

If you're a probate attorney or legal professional and notice any inaccuracies or areas for improvement, I welcome your insights. Please email me at angel@properprobate.guide. Your feedback will help ensure this guide remains accurate, accessible, and helpful for everyone who needs it.

—Dr. Angelique C. Hamane

Glossary of Terms

Administrator: A person appointed by the court to manage the estate when there is no will (intestate) or no named executor.

Attorney General: The state's chief legal officer responsible for representing the public interest, including overseeing charitable trusts and unclaimed property.

Beneficiary: A person or entity entitled to receive assets from a will, trust, or estate.
See also: Heir.

Breach of Fiduciary Duty: When a trustee or executor fails to act in the best interests of the beneficiaries or fails to follow the terms of the trust or will.

Court Filing: The act of submitting legal documents to the court. Must be done using the proper method—e-filing, in person, or by mail—based on local rules.

Decedent: The person who has passed away, leaving behind a trust or estate.
See also: Grantor, Testator, Trustor.

Estate: All the property, assets, and liabilities left by the decedent.

Evidentiary Rulings: Court decisions that determine whether a particular piece of evidence is admissible or inadmissible during a trial or hearing. These rulings are made in response to objections and are based on legal standards, including relevance, hearsay rules, and other evidentiary principles.

Executor: The person named in a will to carry out the decedent's instructions and manage the estate.
Also called: Personal Representative.

Fee Waiver: A request submitted to the court to waive filing fees due to financial hardship.

Fiduciary: A person legally obligated to act in the best interests of others, such as a trustee or executor.

Filing Fee: The required payment to submit legal documents to the court.
See also: Fee Waiver.

Financial Elder Abuse: The exploitation of an elder's assets through coercion, manipulation, or fraud.

Fraud: Intentional deception that causes someone to act against their interests—such as signing a document under false pretenses.

Grantor: The person who creates a trust and transfers assets into it. After death, the grantor becomes the decedent, and the trust becomes irrevocable.
Also known as: Settlor, Trustor.

Heir: A person who inherits property under California's intestacy laws when there is no valid will or trust.
See also: Beneficiary.

Interested Party: Anyone who has a legal interest in the outcome of a probate case, such as a beneficiary, heir, or trustee.

Lack of Capacity: A legal term used when someone did not understand what they were signing—often due to dementia, illness, or cognitive decline.

Local Rules: The specific procedural rules adopted by a county court that apply in addition to state laws and the California Rules of Court.

Mandatory Settlement Conference (MSC): A court-ordered meeting where parties attempt to resolve their dispute with the assistance of a neutral judge or settlement officer.

Motion: A formal request made to the court, asking the judge to issue an order or make a ruling on a specific issue before or during trial. Common types include **motions to dismiss**, **motions for summary judgment**, and **motions in limine**.

Notice of Hearing: A document that informs interested parties of the date, time, and location of an upcoming court hearing.

Notice of Trust Administration: A formal notice (required under Probate Code § 16061.7) that informs heirs and beneficiaries of the existence of a trust and their right to contest it within 120 days.
Also known as: 120-Day Rule.

Objection: A formal response filed by someone who opposes the petition or action being requested in court.

Petition: A legal document filed with the court to request judicial action—such as challenging a trust, removing a trustee, or requesting an accounting.

Petitioner: The person who files the petition and initiates the court case.
Also known as: Moving Party.

Pleading Paper: A legal format required by many courts. It includes numbered lines down the left margin to help the court cite specific parts of the document.

Private Mediation: A voluntary process where parties hire a professional mediator to facilitate settlement discussions, often chosen for flexibility and confidentiality.

Probate Notes: Internal memos prepared by the court that identify problems with the petition, such as missing documents or service issues. These must be cleared before the hearing.

Proof of Service: A document confirming that all required parties were properly served with legal notice. Must be filed with the court.

Prudent Investor Rule: A legal standard that requires trustees to manage and invest trust assets with care, skill, and caution, balancing risk and reward while maintaining financial stability.

Respondent: The person or party who responds to the petition. In trust litigation, this is often the acting trustee or a beneficiary being challenged.

Self-dealing: The act of a fiduciary using trust assets for personal gain or making decisions that benefit themselves at the expense of the estate.

Service of Notice: The act of delivering legal documents to interested parties in the proper manner (e.g., by mail, personal service, or publication).

Standing: The legal right to file a case in court. In probate, this typically means being an heir, beneficiary, or otherwise directly affected by the outcome.

Summons: A formal court document notifying the respondent that a case has been filed and that they are required to respond. *Form DE-125.*

Trust: A legal arrangement in which one party (the trustee) holds and manages property for the benefit of another (the beneficiary).

Trustee: The person or entity responsible for administering the trust according to its terms and in the best interests of the beneficiaries.
Also known as: Fiduciary.

Legal Grounds and Related Codes

Lack of Capacity
Probate Code § 810 — Presumption of capacity unless proven otherwise
Probate Code § 811 — Guidelines for determining mental capacity
Probate Code § 812 — Requirements for capacity to make a decision

Undue Influence
Welfare and Institutions Code § 15610.70 — Definition and criteria for undue influence
Probate Code § 86 — Definition related to undue influence in elder abuse
Probate Code § 259 — Disqualification from inheritance due to undue influence
Probate Code § 17200 — Challenging a trust based on undue influence
Estate of Sarabia (1990) 221 Cal. App. 3d 599 — Legal standards for undue influence

Financial Elder Abuse
Welfare and Institutions Code § 15610.27 — Definition of "Elder.
Welfare and Institutions Code § 15610.30 — Financial abuse of elders and dependent adults
Probate Code § 259 — Disqualification of abusers from inheriting

Breach of Fiduciary Duty
Probate Code § 16000 — Duty of loyalty
Probate Code § 16004 — Conflict of interest involving trustees
Probate Code § 16047 — Prudent investment of trust assets
Probate Code § 16060 — Duty to inform and account to beneficiaries
Probate Code § 16062 — Requirement for periodic accounting

Andersen v. Hunt (2011) 196 Cal.App.4th 722 — Fiduciary duty and trustee misconduct

Fraud

Probate Code § 850 — Petitions involving fraud or property disputes
Code of Civil Procedure § 2015.5 — Verification under penalty of perjury
Hegseth v. Superior Court (2017) 10 Cal.App.5th 360 — Contesting a trust based on fraud

Improper Execution

Probate Code § 8252 — Contesting the validity of a will
Rules of Court, Rule 7.104 — Petition content requirements
Rules of Court, Rule 2.105 — Formatting standards (pleading paper)

Misappropriation or Mismanagement of Assets

Probate Code § 16000 — Management of estate assets
Probate Code § 16004 — Avoiding conflicts of interest
Probate Code § 16047 — Prudent management of assets
Probate Code § 16060 — Informing beneficiaries
Probate Code § 16062 — Accounting for estate assets

References

California Probate Code
§ 48 - Definition of "interested person" for contesting a trust or will.
§ 86 - Definition of a small estate.
§ 259 - Disqualification of persons who abuse the decedent from inheriting.
§§ 810-812 - General provisions on mental capacity.
§ 850 - Petitions to determine the rights of parties to property.
§ 1215 - Service of notice by mail.
§ 1220 - Proof of service.
§§ 1219-1220 - Requirements for notice and proof of notice.
§§ 6400 et seq., 2024 - Intestate succession and distribution of assets.
§ 8004(b) - Deadlines for filing a will contest after admission to probate.
§ 8252 - Contesting a will.
§ 10810 (2025) - Statutory fee calculation for probate attorneys.
§ 13100 - Small Estate Affidavit procedure.
§ 13200 (2025) - Affidavit procedures for small estates with real property.
§§ 16000-16015 - Duties of trustees, including care and management of trust assets.
§ 16000 - Duty of loyalty.
§ 16004 - Conflict of interest for trustees.
§ 16047 - Duty of prudent investment.
§ 16060 - Duty to inform and account to beneficiaries.
§ 16062 - Requirement for periodic accounting.
§ 16061.7 - Notification of Trust Administration requirements.
§ 16061.8 - Deadline for filing a petition contesting a living trust.
§ 17200 - Grounds for petitioning the court regarding trusts.

California Rules of Court
Rule 2.105 - Requirement for court documents on pleading paper.

Rule 2.107 - Formatting standards for documents.
Rule 2.111 - Requirements for the first page of court documents.
Rule 2.111(1) - Case caption requirements.
Rule 2.111(3) - Information to include on the first page.
Rules 2.100-2.119 - Format and filing requirements for court documents.
Rules 2.250-2.261 - Electronic filing and service requirements.
Rule 2.257 - Signature requirements for electronically filed documents.
Rule 3.1110(f) - Requirements for exhibits in motions.
Rule 3.1110(f)(4) - Indexing of exhibits.
Rule 3.1380 - Mandatory Settlement Conference (MSC) guidelines.
Rule 3.55 - Waiver of court fees.
Rule 7.104 - Contents of a petition for probate.

California Code of Civil Procedure

§ 474 - Naming defendants when identity is unknown.
§ 1985 - Issuing subpoenas.
§ 2015.5 - Verification under penalty of perjury.
§ 2025.010 - Conducting depositions.
§ 2030.010 - Form Interrogatories.
§ 2031.010 - Request for the Production of Documents.
§ 2033.010 - Requests for Admissions

California Welfare and Institutions Code

§ 15610.27 - Definition of "Elder."
§ 15610.30 - Financial abuse of elders and dependent adults.
§ 15610.70 - Legal criteria for proving undue influence.

California Government Code

§ 68630 - Fee Waivers in Civil and Probate Cases.

Case Law

Andersen v. Hunt (2011) 196 Cal.App.4th 722 - Breach of fiduciary duty and trustee misconduct.

Barefoot v. Jennings (2020) 8 Cal.5th 822 - Standing for disinherited beneficiaries to contest trusts due to fraud, undue influence, or lack of capacity.

Estate of Lind (1989) 209 Cal.App.3d 1424: Addressed the rights of disinherited heirs to challenge a will based on prior valid estate planning documents, emphasizing standing as an heir if the will is deemed invalid.

Estate of Sarabia (1990) 221 Cal. App. 3d 599 - Legal standards for undue influence in probate.

Estate of Simmonds (1972) 6 Cal.3d 525: Clarified that disinherited heirs may have standing if they would inherit under intestacy, should the will be declared invalid.

Smith (2023) - Guidelines for undue influence in probate cases.

List of Tables and Figures

Tables

Table 1.1. Wills vs. Trusts
Table 1.2. Common Misconceptions About Wills vs. Trusts
Table 1.3. Probate vs. Trust Administration: Key Differences
Table 1.4. Procedural Differences Between Probate and Trust Administration
Table 1.5. Key Players in the Probate Process
Table 2.1. Trial Stages
Table 5.1. Common Legal Grounds for Contesting a Trust or Will
Table 6.1. Statutory Fees (California)
Table 6.2. Estimated Probate Litigation Costs (California)
Table 6.3. Contingency Representation
Table 7.1. Procedural Compliance vs. Legal Content
Table 8.1. Sample Timeline of Events
Table 8.2. Commonly Cited California Statutory Codes
Table 9.1. How California Probate Code Defines Mental Capacity
Table 10.1: Legal Heading Levels and Formatting Guide
Table 10.2. Common Legal Role Labels in a Probate Petition
Table 10.3. Required Probate Forms (California)

Figures

Figure 1.1. Assets That Bypass Probate
Figure 1.2. Key Takeaways – Understanding Probate
Figure 2.1. Key Steps in a Probate Dispute
Figure 2.2. Timeline of Filings and Court Appearances
Figure 2.3. Key Takeaways – Steps Toward Trial

Figure 3.1. Filing Deadline Example
Figure 3.2. Key Takeaways – Understanding Deadlines
Figure 4.1. Who Qualifies as an "Interested Person" Under California Probate Code § 48.
Figure 4.2. Key Takeaways – Who Has Standing?
Figure 5.1. The Four Elements of Undue Influence
Figure 5.2. Types of Evidence to Support Claim
Figure 5.3. Evaluating the Strength of Your Case
Figure 5.4. Key Takeaways – Building a Strong Case
Figure 6.1. Key Takeaways – Going It Alone
Figure 7.1. Key Steps to Filing a Probate Petition
Figure 7.2. Key Takeaways – Filing Process
Figure 8.1. Examples of Clear and Effective Court Titles
Figure 8.2. Written Narrative of Key Events
Figure 8.3. Key Takeaways – Legal Content
Figure 9.1. Checklist: Signs of Vulnerability
Figure 9.2. Checklist: Signs of Apparent Authority
Figure 9.3. Checklist: Signs of Actions and Tactics Used
Figure 9.4. Checklist: Signs of Inequity of the Result
Figure 9.5. Key Takeaways – Legal Grounds
Figure 10.1. Sample 28-Line Pleading Paper
Figure 10.2. Sample Title Page with Annotations
Figure 10.3. Sample Heading Structure for a Petition
Figure 10.4. Sample Paragraph Numbering and Indentation
Figure 10.5. Sample Footer with Title and Page Number
Figure 10.6. Sample Petition Referencing Exhibit A
Figure 10.7. Sample Exhibit Cover Page for Attachments
Figure 10.8. Headers for Required Court Forms
Figure 10.9. Probate Case Cover Sheet – PRO-010
Figure 10.10. Summons Form – DE-125
Figure 10.11. Notice of Hearing Form – DE-120
Figure 10.12. Proof of Service Form DE-120(P)
Figure 10.13. Example of Verification Statement
Figure 10.14 Comparison of Wet and Electronic Signatures
Figure 10.15. Example of an Organized Filing System
Figure 10.16. Key Takeaways – Technical Requirements

Figure 11.1. Service Summary List
Figure 11.2. Step-by-Step Guide to Filing and Serving a Probate Petition
Figure 11.3. Key Takeaways – Filing a Petition.

Final Thoughts: Moving Forward with Confidence

Navigating the probate process can feel overwhelming—but you've already taken the first important step by educating yourself and preparing to move forward. As you continue on this journey, stay persistent, stay organized, and don't hesitate to seek support when needed.

I created this guide to make the process more manageable, and I hope it has given you practical tools and the confidence to advocate for your rights in probate court.

If you'd like more guidance, I offer **free and low-cost online courses**, downloadable templates, and additional tools to support you at every stage. For those looking for more comprehensive, step-by-step support, a full flagship course is also available.

 Visit **www.properprobate.guide** to access free resources, stay connected for updates, and explore support options that fit your needs.

Thank you for allowing me to be part of your journey. Your determination to face probate on your own is both courageous and inspiring. Wishing you strength, clarity, and success as you move forward.

www.ingramcontent.com/pod-product-compliance
Lightning Source LLC
Chambersburg PA
CBHW051353290426
44108CB00015B/1994